PATRICK BARLOW

Patrick Barlow has been an actor, director and writer for theatre, film, television and radio since 1970. After creating and performing in a number of street, community and children's theatres across the country, he formed the National Theatre of Brent in 1981.

Celebrated for its two-man comedy epic theatre, the NToB has appeared in the UK and Europe in theatre, television and radio. Their many subjects include *The Charge of the Light Brigade*, *Wagner's Ring*, *The Charles and Diana Story*, *The Messiah*, *The Wonder of Sex*, *The Arts and How They Was Done*, *The Life and Times of the Dalai Lama*, *Massive Landmarks of the Twentieth Century*, *The Black Hole of Calcutta* and *Zulu!* They have won two Sony Gold Awards for Best Radio Comedy, a Premier Ondas Award for Best European Comedy, and the New York Festival Gold Award for Best Comedy.

The Messiah was originally written on the island of Iona off Mull, then developed with Julian Hough and Jude Kelly, and first performed at the Battersea Arts Centre, then the Tricycle Theatre, London, in 1983. *The Messiah* has seen Patrick work with many illustrious collaborators, including Jim Broadbent, Robert Austin, Tom Cairns, John Ramm and Martin Duncan. It was rewritten with John Ramm for the Bush in 1999 and directed by Loveday Ingram. The current NToB is Patrick, John and Martin Duncan whose collaboration is now time-honoured and long-standing. The latest version of *The Messiah* is a return to the very first 1983 Tricycle version.

Besides the NToB, Patrick adapted John Buchan's *The 39 Steps* which played in the West End for nine years, and over forty countries worldwide. It has won Olivier, Tony, Helpmann and Molière Awards and made Patrick the most performed playwright in America for 2012/13.

Other plays include his new version of *A Christmas Carol* which opened off-Broadway in 2015, and in the UK in 2016 at the Noël Coward Theatre with Jim Broadbent as Scrooge, and was nominated for an Olivier Award in 2017. Other plays include his four-person *Ben-Hur* (Tricycle, 2015), his adaptation of John Milton's *Comus* (Shakespeare's Globe, 2017) and *How to Deal with Being Dumped: A Marital Oratorio* (Gogmagogs and North American tour, 1999).

Patrick's screenwriting includes *The Growing Pains of Adrian Mole*, *Christopher Columbus*, *Queen of the East*, *Van Gogh* (Prix Futura Berlin Film Festival), *Revolution!!* (Best Comedy Jerusalem Film Festival) and the BAFTA-winning *The Young Visiters*.

Publications include *Shakespeare: The Truth!* and *The Complete History of the Whole World*.

Screen and theatre acting credits include *A Funny Thing Happened on the Way to the Forum*, *Loot*, *Wind in the Willows* (National Theatre), *Absolutely Fabulous*, *French and Saunders*, *Jam and Jerusalem*, *Shakespeare in Love*, *Notting Hill*, *Bridget Jones*, *Nanny McPhee* and *A Very English Scandal*.

Patrick Barlow

THE MESSIAH

With additional material by
Julian Hough, Jude Kelly and John Ramm

NICK HERN BOOKS
London
www.nickhernbooks.co.uk

A Nick Hern Book

The Messiah first published in Great Britain in 2001 as a paperback original by Nick Hern Books Limited, The Glasshouse, 49a Goldhawk Road, London W12 8QP

This new revised edition published in 2018

The Messiah copyright © 2001, 2018 Patrick Barlow
Foreword copyright 2018 Patrick Barlow

Patrick Barlow has asserted his moral right to be identified as the author of this work

Front cover: Feast Creative

Designed and typeset by Nick Hern Books, London
Printed in the UK by Mimeo Ltd, Huntingdon, Cambridgeshire PE29 6XX

ISBN 978 1 84842 807 2

A CIP catalogue record for this book is available from the British Library

Foreword
Patrick Barlow

I wrote the first draft of *The Messiah* on the island of Iona, just off Mull in the Scottish Highlands. Someone told me it might be a good place to write a Nativity play.

Iona was where St Columba arrived in 563 to convert the heathen Picts. Nowadays there is a proper ferry with a restaurant, lounges and car deck, but in 1982 only a small motorboat could make the journey and only when the sea wasn't rough. I took the long trip in November when the seas were wild and far-off lightning criss-crossed the sky. Already I'd spent two nights in a B&B in Fionnphort, waiting for the tide to drop and gazing at the grey stone abbey and pure white sands of Iona tantalisingly in the distance. The white black-rocked sands where sixty-eight monks were massacred by Vikings on Christmas Eve in 986. It is still called Martyrs Bay. The massacred monks, they say, made the great work of illuminated gospels, the Manuscript of Columba, or Book of Kells.

The seas dropped sufficiently and the little pale blue boat arrived to take us across the churning waters of Iona Sound to the island. We pulled ourselves aboard and the driver helped lug my heavy case of books into the bottom of the boat. As I jumped in I saw a nun, grey and white-robed, in green wellies, staring at me with a broad jaw and determined look.

'What are you doing here?' she demanded. 'What on earth's in these ridiculous heavy cases?'
'They're books for a play I'm writing,' I replied.
'How many books?'
'Heaps.'
'Play about what?'
'A kind of – '
'What?'

'Nativity play,' I replied to the deep brown eyes.
'Well you won't need books for that.'
'Won't I?'
'The island will give you everything.'
'What will it give me?'
She held on to her flapping habit as the outboard spluttered and
the little boat lurched and swung out towards the island.
I thought she hadn't heard.
I said again: 'What will it give me?'
She stared out to the island then back to me.
She said: 'The veil is very thin on Iona.'
The boat lurched. We clung to the sides. Spray hit our faces.
Was she talking to me?
'Sorry, I don't understand.'
She looked at me rather puzzled. She said it again. Emphasising
each word with clear-cut precision:

'The
veil
is
very
thin
on
Iona.'

I tried to write my play. I spent days at it. I battled through my
books and got nowhere. Every afternoon, in the fading light,
I marched round the island listening to my brand-new Walkman
cassette player. I had two cassettes. Handel's *Messiah* which I'd
never heard before. Particularly 'Comfort Ye My People' which
I played over and over and over, my boots sinking into the sodden
turf. The other cassette I bought at the Oban gift shop. This was
The Best of Ossian. Particularly 'The Road to Drumleman' which
I played over and over and over too. I marched on, leaning into
the stinging wind, sloshing my feet in time to the music.

One day on a bright early morning, the sister came knocking at
my door.
'How's your play going?'
'Very very hard,' I replied. 'I don't know where I am.'

'Come along.'

'What?'

'We're going for a walk!'

'But I haven't even – '

'No "but I haven't even"s! Come along, boots on. Waterproof zipped. I'm showing you the island. You'll never write anything if you don't see the island.'

We walked in the bright cold sun and she showed me the island. She showed me the green marble cliffs of Iona. We collected pieces of green marble from the white beaches. She showed me Columba's Bay where Columba first landed, dragging his tiny vessel high on to the sand. She pointed west across the leaping sea to his home in Ireland. She told me how he'd been a high prince who fought a terrible war in Ulster, resulting in the deaths of many. He sought repentance for all the blood he'd spilt and that night heard a voice in a dream. He must fashion a coracle from wood and skins and row his way east across the sea till he could no longer see his Irish home. He must settle where he landed but never return. Only then could he be forgiven.

Columba's coracle, she said, was like a large upturned walnut and he pushed on his single oar, beating his way across the waves. He looked back but still saw Ireland bobbing in the distance. At long last he reached a low white island and landed there amongst the green marble just as dawn was rising. Leaving his craft on the green stone strand, he climbed to the topmost point of the island, the mount of Dun I. He stood in the first morning light amongst the swooping gulls. He looked back across the creeping churning seas, but no Ireland came to view.

He was forgiven.

I looked across the sea and marvelled at the distance.

'How did he get all the way here from Ireland in a tiny boat with one oar?'

'He didn't give up,' she replied with a flinty look.

On the same day, she showed me the Hermit's Cell – a circle of stones reputed to be the foundations of Columba's own cell, open to the sky, the elements and the whirling stars where he went alone to pray, she said. Sometimes on our walk she would pray herself, but not all alone like Columba. We marched in the bright sun and the wind skimmed cold on our faces and she sang and prayed aloud to her Lord like a companion.

'Oh thank you, thank you, dear Father, for all THIS. For the grey rocks, for the green green moss, for the whistling wind that sings, for the frosty white islands strung out like pearls along the horizon.'

At one point she stopped and said 'Right! We'll have our sandwiches here', and she produced two brown-paper bags, one for each of us. She sat on a rock and said grace then began to eat while I leapt up a strange-shaped black cliff face, strangely placed in the middle of the flat emerald moor. I clambered to the top of the black rock, catching my breath and exhiliarated. I stood up to get a view. Then a voice from below. A voice without mercy, like a maths mistress. Or more like my mother.

'WHAT ARE YOU DOING UP THERE? Come down this instant! Do you have any idea what that cliff is?'

'No,' I replied from the top, feeling inexplicably guilty.

'The druids sacrificed their victims from there. They cut their throats and threw them from the top. It's full of bad spirits. Come down immediately, do you hear!'

I came down immediately.

That same night, I woke screaming from nightmares. I forced myself awake so they wouldn't return.

I told the sister next day.

'Well I did tell you,' she said.

The sky began to golden on the distant line of horizon and she scrambled us to the top of Dun I to find the Well of Eternal Youth.

We stood with views to all four compass points. Below us the Bay at the Back of the Ocean. Next stop America. The island of Staffa far out like a moored boat. Or a whale. Waiting for the tide to take it. We could see the white ribs and black mouth of

Fingal's Cave. The waves foaming in and out, boiling in circles.
She pointed to a perfectly formed hill, like a burial mound. The
Hill of Angels she said. Where one night Columba was followed
by a single curious monk – 'Strictly against orders, naughty
man!' – to discover the saint on top of the hill, hands raised and
dancing beneath the stars, surrounded by a ring of golden-winged
angels. Also dancing. We laughed at the idea. The dancing saint
and the dancing angels and the little monk, wide-eyed, watching
beneath the moon. His life changed for ever.

'Look at the sea,' she shouted through the thundering wind.
I pulled up my green waterproof, the zip against my teeth, and
lifted my glasses spattered by rain.
'What colour is it?' she commanded.
'What?' I shouted back.
'The sea! The sea!'
I peered down at the shifting waves. I cleaned my glasses.
'Grey,' I replied.
'Grey? *Grey!?*' she shouted back. 'Are you colour blind! Look
look! The seas of Iona are *not* grey! They are a myriad of all
God's colours, blues and greens, jade, topaz and amethyst.
Can't you see them!'

She sounded hurt. I squinted through the stinging rain and
looked for God's colours.

'Deeper! Look deeper!' she shouted through the thunder.

To drink the water in the Well of Eternal Youth we had to bend
deep to our knees, hang on to a rock and reach down with our
free hands to break the still, black surface. We cupped the water
in our curling hands. When it finally reached our lips, the taste
was icy cold and sweet. There was salt in the wind and the wind
sang round us.

We returned from the island on the same day as the dawn was
breaking. We had been there one week. I clambered out of the
boat, lugging my cases after me. She was no longer in wellies
but in smart leather shoes. Her grey habit was clean and
pressed. She told me the convent founder chose habits of grey
and not black so as not to frighten children.

The Iona Sound was still as we rode home.We travelled by bus through the early light of Mull and said goodbye at Oban. The seagulls screeched about us. She said, 'Oh be quiet, you silly things!'

I wanted to hug her but I didn't. We shook hands.

She said, 'Goodbye then and God bless you.'

She took another bus to her convent in Aberdeen, I caught the train to Glasgow and on to London.

I went to Iona hoping to come back with a play. I came back with a notebook full of sketches and bits of dialogue, an early birth scene, based on memories of my son Sam's birth, and a God and Gabriel scene that has remained unchanged since the start.

The journey of *The Messiah* has been a long one. A thirty-five-year journey. It has been filmed, recorded and staged in the UK, Europe, Australia and New Zealand. It has been revised, revived, rewritten and rewritten again. The latest version, the version in this book is the closest to the first version. The Iona version.

I have been blessed with many companions and collaborators on this journey, all of whom I sincerely trust I properly acknowledge in this volume.

Many companions and collaborators. But the first, without doubt and without parallel, my navigator, storyteller, protector from bad spirits, my flinty-eyed guide across the rocks, streams and strands of Iona where my play was imagined, conceived and born.

My sister in green wellies from Aberdeen. Her words still ringing through the wind on the bouncing boat from Fionnphort.

The
veil
is
very
thin
on
Iona.

November 2018

This new production of *The Messiah* was first performed at the Birmingham Repertory Theatre on 18 October 2018, and subsequently performed at the New Theatre, Cardiff, the Lyceum Theatre, Sheffield, the Cheltenham Everyman Theatre, Richmond Theatre, and The Other Palace, London. The cast was as follows:

MAURICE ROSE	Hugh Dennis
RONALD BREAM	John Marquez
MRS LEONORA FFLYTE	Lesley Garrett
MRS LEONORA FFLYTE ALTERNATE	Margaret Preece
MALE ROLES UNDERSTUDY	Adam Morris

Director	Patrick Barlow
Associate Director	Tom Latter
Designer	Francis O'Connor
Lighting Designer	Howard Hudson
Sound Designer	Bobby Aitken
Choreographer	Siân Williams

The original version of *The Messiah* was performed at the Tricycle Theatre, London, in January 1983, with the following cast:

Patrick Barlow
Julian Hough
Lee Trevorrow

Director	Jude Kelly
Designer	Tom Cairns

Acknowledgements

Although this version of *The Messiah* is not a National Theatre
of Brent production, all previous UK versions of the play, since
1982, have been. They have all been blessed with invaluable
collaborations from performers, directors and designers and
I want to honour and thank them all in this edition. I pray I have
missed out nobody. Besides the wonderful creatives and company
of the current production, I want to thank all previous *Messiah*
creatives: Julian Hough, Lee Trevorrow, Jude Kelly, Tom Cairns,
Jim Broadbent, Michael Minas, Anastasia Broadbent, Robert
Austin, John Ramm, Kate Flowers, Susan Flannery, Loveday
Ingram, Peter Lindley, Anthony Van Laast and Martin Duncan.

P.B.

Dedicated to
The Isle of Iona
Where this began

Characters

The Messiah is written for two actors and an opera singer

ACTOR ONE – MAURICE ROSE
ACTOR TWO – RONALD BREAM
SINGER – LEONORA 'MRS F' FFLYTE

The text published here may differ slightly from the play as performed in the 2018 production.

ACT ONE

Stage – general

A circular (revolving) stage. Three tall classical columns and broken shorter columns surround it. Behind the columns, midnight-blue drapes with gold stars. By the stage-right column an elegant and plush dining-room chair.

Music: Handel – 'Hallelujah'.

Enter MAURICE ROSE *and* RONALD BREAM *through the midnight-blue drapes. They stand imposingly centre-stage. The music plays. And plays.* RONALD *looks alarmed.* MAURICE *signals offstage to turn it off.*

Music cuts abruptly.

MAURICE. Picture – if you will – in as it were the mind's eye – the lone figure of a –

RONALD (*sotto*). I haven't got the chair.

MAURICE. What?

RONALD (*sotto*). I haven't got the chair.

MAURICE (*sotto*). Then get the chair, Ronald.

RONALD *turns towards* MRS F*'s chair.*

That's Mrs F's chair! Chair, Ronald!

RONALD *exits hurriedly.* MAURICE *looks awkwardly at the audience. A huge clattering offstage.* RONALD *returns, limping slightly. He carries a fold-up chair. Opens it, pinches his finger. Positions it.* MAURICE *continues.*

– in as it were the mind's eye – the lone figure of a man. Entirely alone in the great vastness of the desert.

RONALD *stands on the chair.*

Lights change.

Desert – night

MAURICE. See! How he stands! His brilliant black eyes
restlessly roving the face of the universe searching into the
depths of the heavens for the sign that he is looking for.

RONALD*'s eyes restlessly rove.*

Upon his head he wears a crown, a moon upon its left side,
a sun upon its right; about his shoulders a jewel-encrusted
cloak; a silken robe of aquamarine girds his loins.

RONALD *mimes awkwardly.*

About his wrists, bracelets in the shape of sand-snakes;
a mighty jewel hangs heavy upon his index finger.

RONALD *sticks out a middle finger.*

Index finger!

RONALD *sticks out index finger.*

He is an Wise Man from the Orient. He is a thousand
years old.

RONALD *plays very old.*

He knows the secrets of the earth, he has heard the music of
the spheres and has gazed upon the etheric web of his own
astral body.

RONALD *awkwardly puts his hands over his crotch.*

He stands now, as he has stood night after night, eyes fixed
upon the stars, entirely motionless.

MAURICE *stands motionless for twenty-five seconds.*

RONALD *waits awkwardly. His legs start to tremble. He
looks panicked.*

Suddenly – a light appears in the sky. A new light. A star –
hitherto unseen through the history of stars. 'It is the sign
I been looking for,' he mutters beneath his breath as he –

RONALD (*mutters*). It is the sign I been looking for!

MAURICE. – as he leaps upon his milk-white dromedary –

RONALD *leaps on to his imaginary dromedary.*

– and grasps the silken reins. The proud beast rises proudly up –

RONALD *and the dromedary rise up.*

– and bears him across the Syrian dunes towards the glinting golden minarets of his far distant palace.

RONALD (*à la Lawrence of Arabia*). Hut-hut! Hut-hut! Hut-hut!

RONALD *gallops round the stage and exits. Immediately re-enters. He gallops to the chair and shoots offstage with it.*

Another clattering.

Stage – general

MAURICE. Thank you. But now some introductions –

RONALD *re-enters, limping.*

I am Maurice Bromsgrove Rose, the Founder and Artistic Director of the Maurice Rose Players and very much the maison d'être, if you will, of the company's artistic policies.

Hello.

And this is my associate and – Full Acting Company Ronald Bream –

Nods to RONALD.

RONALD. Yes. Thank you. I am Ronald Ricardo Bream and I am more than pleased and dishonoured to be here to be tonight acting tonight here with the Maurice Rose Players.

MAURICE (*sotto*). Hello.

RONALD (*to him*). Hello.

MAURICE. No – (*Say hello to audience.*) Hello.

RONALD (*to audience*). Hello.

MAURICE. And now it is our honour and privilege to introduce to you our special guest star here this evening. Singing some of the greatest arias from the Handel Messiah and many other Messiahs also, please welcome Mrs Leonora Fflyte.

Fanfare.

They turn to the blue drapes which swish open. A light comes up. Nothing happens.

RONALD. She's not there, Maurice!

MAURICE. I can see that, Ronald.

MAURICE *signals. The tabs close.*

Mrs Leonora Fflyte.

Repeat fanfare.

The blue drapes swish open again. Still nothing happens.

RONALD. She's not there again, Maurice!

MAURICE. Thank you, Ronald.

MAURICE *signals. The tabs close.*

Just go and get her, please.

RONALD. I can't do that, Maurice. It's like a labyrinth back there!

MAURICE (*laughing with the audience*). It's only 'backstage', Ronald!!

RONALD (*shouting off*). Mrs F!!

MAURICE. Ronald!!

(*To audience.*) Dear oh dear! Not very 'used to the theatre', are you, Ronald?

(*Laughing.*) So – ladies and gentlemen – whilst we 'await the appearance' of our special guest star here this evening – Mrs Leonora Fflyte –

RONALD. Mrs F.

MAURICE. Mrs – F – let us now without further or 'much' ado –

MAURICE *laughs knowingly.* RONALD *laughs too. No idea what he's laughing at.*

– begin the telling of our ancient and ne'er to be forgot tale of tales here this evening. Thank you, Ronald.

(*Sotto.*) Thank you, Maurice.

RONALD. You're Maurice.

MAURICE. No. Thank you, *Maurice*!

RONALD. Ah yes! Thank you, 'Maurice'. So now – ladies and gentlemen – let us begin now begin our show here this evening by moving – back, back and forth in time and on and up, up to those higher climes of cosmic domicile where the high and mighty celestial powers wrestle with the earth's trousers.

MAURICE. Traumas!

RONALD. It's trousers!

MAURICE. Traumas!

RONALD. It said trousers. I been working on trousers.

MAURICE. I'm hardly going to write 'The Earth's Trousers' am I Ronald?

RONALD. I don't know!

MAURICE. The Earth's Traumas!

RONALD. The Earth's Traumas!

MAURICE. Rock!

RONALD. I beg your pardon?

MAURICE. ROCK!

RONALD. Right! Thank you.

RONALD *exits. Then re-enters, staggering with the cosmic rock, which he drops in place.* MAURICE *ascends the rock as* GOD.

Lights change.

Heavenly realms

MAURICE. Gabriel O Gabriel. O my most-favoured seraph. Come forth!

Enter RONALD *as the* ARCHANGEL GABRIEL. *He raises his arms as angel wings.*

GABRIEL. Hello, Godhead.

GOD. Hello.

GABRIEL. Hello.

GOD. Hello.

They do a choreographed movement to each other.

GABRIEL. As you know I am Gabriel. Your most-flavoured seraph –

GOD. No – not flav–

GABRIEL. – and whinging messenger.

GOD. No, not whinging is he?!

GABRIEL. Isn't he?

GOD. No! Wing-ed! Wing-ed messenger!

GABRIEL. Wing-en-ed-ed message – messenge –

GOD. Wing-ed messenger!

GABRIEL. Wing-in-ed messagy windy whingey ginger minge –

GOD (*shocked*). *Ronald!*

GABRIEL. *What?*

GOD. WING-ED! WING-ED!

GABRIEL. I'm sayin' it, aren't I! Christ!

GOD (*ignores*). So Gabriel –

GABRIEL. Yes O Most Ineffinable Being?

GOD. Have you visited the Earth? She whom I love? Recently?

GABRIEL. I have as it happens, O Father of the Sky.

GOD. So – does the Earth, does she send me 'word'?

GABRIEL. Um – well – put it like this.

GOD. Yes?

GABRIEL. The Earth –

GOD. Yes?

GABRIEL. – is in torment.

GOD. Torment?

GABRIEL. Her weeping rends the air.

GOD. Weeping? Wherefore does she weep? Is she not cared for?

GABRIEL. By the stones, by the trees by the grass, by every creeping thing she is cared for. Bar one… creeping thing.

GOD. Bar one?

GABRIEL. Bar one.

GOD. What?

GABRIEL. Humans.

GOD. Humans?

GABRIEL. Human beings!

GOD. Human beings!!! But they arose from her mud and danced!

GABRIEL. That's all changed now.

GOD. But they placed her stones in circles, they conversed with eagles, they sang to the sea.

GABRIEL. Yes – they did.

GOD. And they don't now?

GABRIEL. No. They murder whales now.

GOD. Oh no!!! Do none love her? Like what I do – love her?

GABRIEL. No. Well – a few. Women mainly. The men go into the darkness generally and go mad. They've got leaders.

GOD. Leaders?

GABRIEL. Herod the Great, Caesar Augustus, Pontius Pilate, Donald – Duck… And the divorce rate is very high as well.

GOD (*in shock*). Where is all the love, Gabriel? The Earth was a gift of love. Where is all the love gone, Gabriel?

GABRIEL. They have not trusted. They have lost the light. They are as in a dark cave. The wind howls across the sea. The waves beat upon the black sand. Dead fish are washed up on the shore. There are no sounds but these. The Earth your lover spins alone through the night. The spirit is gone out of her. The sun has gone.

GOD. Is it too late, O favoured cherubim? Will she die?

GABRIEL. It's hard to say, O Father of the Sky.

GOD. But in your opinion, Gabriel?

GABRIEL. Well, in my opinion, I'd say –

GOD. Yes?

GABRIEL. – there's just time.

GOD. Very well then. We will heal her. We will heal The Earth. We will begin the healing. We will heal her rivers and her seas, her coral reefs, her rocks and her forests, we will heal the white rhino, the flying fish, the hoopoe and the very very rare Himalayan snow leopard. We will heal the souls of people. We will heal their hearts. Their pain and all their severed friendships. We will heal her.

GABRIEL. But how will we heal her, O Lord?

GOD. How will we heal her? We will conceive and we will give birth.

GABRIEL. Give birth?

GOD. Yes.

GABRIEL. And how will we do that precisely?

GOD. What?

GABRIEL. Give birth exactly?

GOD (*not exactly sure*). We will go into the darkness.

GABRIEL. Right?

GOD. Into the darkest most darkenedmost cave will we go –

GABRIEL. Mmm?

GOD. – and we will give birth. To the Sun!

GABRIEL. To the Sun!

GOD. Yes!

GABRIEL. Yes!

GOD. To a great light who shall be there shining in the darkness.

TOGETHER. Let there be light!

Their cosmic fingers move towards each other – à la Michelangelo's God and Adam.

TOGETHER. The Messiah!

Their fingers miss. They aim again.

The Messiah!

Their fingers touch.

SFX: Explosion.

Stage – general

MAURICE. Thank you.

RONALD. Thank you.

MAURICE. And now –

RONALD. Thank you.

MAURICE. Thank you. And now –

RONALD. Yes! And now, ladies and gentlemen, travel with us now down down from those transcendental realms to a little tiny little tiny town –

RONALD *dries.* MAURICE *prompts.*

MAURICE. – in the Roman province of Galilee.

RONALD. In the Roman province of Galilee.

He dries again. MAURICE *prompts.*

MAURICE. Picture if –

RONALD. I know! Picture if you will – in, as it were – the mind's eye –

MAURICE *is muttering the words loudly beside him.*

– the darkened interior of a Syrian dwellin' –

RONALD *can hear* MAURICE *muttering.* RONALD *stops.*

I know the words, Maurice, thank you!

MAURICE. You're doing very well, Ronald.

RONALD. Thank you.

MAURICE. Carry on, Ronald.

RONALD. Thank you! Where our story tonight begins. It is the dwelling of Mary. Rough-hewn white-mud walls that bear no adornment.

MAURICE *mimes rough-hewn white-mud walls.*

Whatchoo doin?

MAURICE. Mimin'.

RONALD. Yes! The embers of a fire give rise to a curling wisp of smoke that ascends to a small opening in the centre of the ceiling –

MAURICE *mimes smoke curling through the roof.*

– a table –

MAURICE *mimes a table.*

– some rough-hewn stools –

MAURICE *mimes stools.*

– and various rough-hewn rudimentary cooking utensils lie upon the dusty floor.

MAURICE *mimes cooking utensils on the floor.*

What's the cutlery doing on the floor? Is she a messy woman?

MAURICE. She's lonely.

RONALD. What, too lonely to tidy up? Is that it?

MAURICE. Quite possibly yes. She's isolated. Never goes out. Lifts've broken down. Phone's off. No friends. She'd leave crockery and cutlery and tea towels and that all over the floors. I'm developing her character, Ronald.

RONALD (*continues*). In the corner a little tiny rough-hewn bed covered with a little tiny rough-hewn blanket and a little tiny rough-hewn pillow.

MAURICE *mimes laying a little blanket on the bed and plumping a little pillow.* RONALD *watches. Resumes.*

Somewhere in the distance a camel barks.

MAURICE *goes behind a pillar. Silence. He does a distant camel impression. Re-emerges.* RONALD *worried.*

Are you alright, Maurice?

MAURICE. Yes thank you. Carry on please.

RONALD. Right. Sitting upon one of the rough-hewn stools is a young rough-hewn girl.

MAURICE. No –

RONALD. What?

MAURICE. Young girl!

RONALD. Young rough-hewn girl!

MAURICE. No!! Young girl!!!

RONALD. Alright!

MAURICE. Thank you, Ronald. Whenever you're ready.

RONALD. Thank you.

MAURICE. Thank you. It is Mary. Sitting all alone. In her little Galiliean home.

Nazareth – Mary's room

RONALD *exits and re-enters with the fold-up chair. He sits. He takes a blue veil which he puts over his head.*

SFX: Mid-Eastern village.

MAURICE. She gazes wistfully into the fire –

    RONALD *gazes wistfully to the right.*

Into the fire!

    RONALD *gazes wistfully to the left.*

Doing her evening sewing.

    RONALD *mimes sewing.*

For Mary is a temple handmaid and sewing is her daily task. She pauses briefly –

    RONALD *pauses.*

– as she gazes down at her handiwork.

    RONALD *gazes down.*

The hem of a seventy-foot temple curtain.

    RONALD *and* MAURICE *both follow the massive length of curtain with their eyes. They gaze miles offstage.*

A knock upon the door startles her far-away thoughts.

    RONALD *looks startled.* MAURICE *stands behind* MARY's *imaginary front door. Raises his hand to knock but there is no actual door. Whispers to a member of the audience.*

Excuse me... would you mind knocking – under your seat. Not yet! In sync with me please. I should have installed a bell. Thank you.

    Audience member does so. MAURICE *walks through the imaginary door.*

RONALD. I haven't said yes yet.

MAURICE *walks out and stands at the imaginary door again.* RONALD *looks startled again.*

MARY. Yes?

MAURICE *enters. He is now* JOSEPH.

JOSEPH. Excuse me?

MARY. Yes? And who are you please?

JOSEPH. I am Joseph. I am working next door.

MARY. Hello.

JOSEPH. Hello.

MARY. What do you do then?

JOSEPH. I am a carpenter.

MARY. I am a lady.

JOSEPH. You are yes.

Awkward moment.

MARY. So what does your – carpeting entail?

JOSEPH. Carpenting.

MARY. Sorry?

JOSEPH. Carpen-ting.

MARY. Car-pent-in' entail?

JOSEPH. Tables, chairs, work surfaces. Small household items. Bread boards. Decorative spice racks.

MARY. Right.

JOSEPH. I would have liked to have made ships. But you don't get a great call on ships in the desert. Apart from camels.

MARY. I beg your pardon?

JOSEPH. Ships of the desert.

Awkward moment.

MARY. I am Mary. I spend my days sitting by the window sewing the temple veil. It is seventy foot long and not what you'd call a picnic.

They follow the length of curtain with their eyes.

I get quite depressed sometimes and I wonder what's the point of it all. In the early mornings I walk in the hills and I dream of all the lands I'd visit if I had the money. Or I'd be a great lady novelist or make fantastic films. I am happiest when I'm walking in the hills. Ponderin'.

JOSEPH. You are very pretty, Mary.

MARY. Thank you very much.

JOSEPH. Um – are you – as yet – betrothed? As is the custom of the time?

MARY. Am I what sorry?

JOSEPH. Betrothed. As is the custom of the time?

MARY. I am not as it happens, no.

JOSEPH. Um – cos – I was wondering could you – would you – be interested in becoming betrothed unto me? With a view to marriage possibly – in the long term?

MARY. Um… (*Thinks.*) Yes, I would be. I would be interested. I think you are very – you have – your eyes are full of sadness.

JOSEPH. Thank you very much. Could you – would you – could you love me?

MARY. Yes. Quite possibly, yes.

JOSEPH. So shall I come round again tomorrow?

MARY. Yes.

JOSEPH. Okay. Bye.

MARY. Bye.

JOSEPH *starts to leave.*

Um –

JOSEPH. Yes?

MARY. I've got a wonky back door. You could mend that while you're here.

JOSEPH. Certainly, Mary. Bye.

MARY. Bye.

MAURICE *mimes closing the door.* MARY *stands.*

MAURICE *back on.*

Stage – general

MAURICE. What do you mean 'wonky back door'?

RONALD. I had an impulse.

MAURICE. Any other 'impulses' you'd like to share with us?

RONALD. Well – I was thinkin' that Mary could have a –

MAURICE. And now, ladies and gentlemen, at this point in the programme, my company and myself would like to briefly halt proceedings in order to explain some of the reasons and intentions behind doing this particular 'oeuvre' here this evening.

RONALD. Particular what?

MAURICE. 'Oeuvre.' In order to engage upon this – dare I say – historic, esoteric and indeed – deeply colonic project, Ronald and myself have undertaken what I can only describe as our own deeply personal personal journeys towards the distant misty chalice of enlightenment. So before we embark further upon our 'show', we have decided to reveal quite candidly the fruits of our journeys – the candid fruits one might say – in order to stand before you tonight fully enlightened, materially unencumbered and entirely naked.

RONALD *surprised. Looks at* MAURICE.

For we have undergone what can only be described as major spiritual journeys of great personal transformation, but also of considerable pain and great personal difficulty. In particular myself. So let us start with myself. And my particular 'journey.' The journey – if you will – of myself.

For I am only recently returned from a long and lifelong search lookin' within myself and into myself to find – myself. All by myself.

So where precisely did I go to find myself and what actually happened in a nutshell? – Well fascinatin'ly my 'journey' began by travellin' deeply into the mystic and shadowy realms of 'Celtic Twilight'. Taking me round virtually all the great 'spiritual centres' of this country, Glastonbury, Stonehenge, the Pilsbury – Ring, the Avebury – thing and of course the maze at Tring. But it was at a secluded monastic retreat just outside the attractive rural town of Hassocks in Sussex that I received possibly the most profoundly enlightening spiritual training that money can buy. Upon my arrival at the monastery, dedicated to the famous silent monk St Placid of Peterborough, the little Brothers of St Placid – dedicated to complete silence – greeted me, silently of course, and took me instantly to their bosoms. They offered me a small bare cell and simple vegan fare. When finally – after months of meditational research in total silent seclusion – I emerged from my darkened cell, in sandals and simple cassock and found myself standing, upon a wide meadow of verdant grasses, before the Father Superior of the monastery, little Brother Bertram who carried with him a vast ancient leather book of his own Secret Teachings. And thus it was we sat together, little Brother Bertram and myself. On tussocks, in Hassocks, in Sussex, in cassocks. And he didst putteth into my hand his vast leather tome and sayeth unto me: 'Maurice Bromsgrove Rose, in my personal opinion you are the most spiritually enlightened being it has ever been mine honour of knowing. Thank you.'

RONALD. I thought they was silent.

MAURICE. Who?

RONALD. The silent monks.

MAURICE. That's right yes they was silent. So –

RONALD. So how'd he say all that then?

MAURICE. Well – um – from – from within. So –

RONALD. Within what?

MAURICE. Himself.

RONALD. So how did you hear it then?

MAURICE. Within – myself.

RONALD *frowns as he takes this in.* MAURICE *waits impatiently. Looks at watch.*

Alright?

RONALD. Yup.

MAURICE. Good. So –

RONALD. So can I do my inner journey now then?

MAURICE. Sorry?

RONALD. My great personal spiritual inner journey of great personal pain and difficulty. Like what you done.

MAURICE. Not sure your spiritual journey was quite as – ha ha – painful or spiritual as –

RONALD. You *said*, Maurice! When we was doin' the workshoppin' of the actin' in your flat, Maurice! In Theydon – what is it?

MAURICE. Bois.

RONALD. Pardon?

MAURICE. Boyz.

RONALD. The workshoppin'! Which I personally found particularly enlight'nin' after my existentstential crisis at the job crisis centre. You said, didn't you, Maurice! Ready, Maurice?

MAURICE. Um –

RONALD (*prompting*). So, Ronald, perhaps you would care to share with us your – your –

MAURICE (*sighs*). Right. Yes. So anyway, Ronald, perhaps you would care to share with us your um –

RONALD. Oh right! Yes! That's right! Yes! Share *my* own personal inner personal pain and spiritual difficulties which I been workshopping on on my own in *my* flat in – in – Knightsbridge?

MAURICE (*surprised*). Knights–

RONALD. Yes. I would actually yes. I would like to share with you. Thank you for reminding me, Maurice. So, ladies and gentlemen, I should now like to briefly halt proceedin's in order to reveal my own personal researches into 'The Body Esperanto Movement' which is my own idea as it happens, as yet unused – or unknown about – by the general 'public', in which the spoken word is replaced by an internationally recognised language of body language to convey our deepest most innermost most personal feelin's which will one day be spoke throughout the world in my opinion. As an example I would now like to show you the past three or four years of mine own personal experiences using only the body language. AKO 'Body Esperanto' which I should now like to share with you now. Thank you.

RONALD *prepares the space. He flexes his knees, shoots his arms out and slaps his face.*

What's that?

MAURICE. Um –

RONALD. Intense loneliness in a room in South London.

MAURICE. Right.

RONALD. And this?

RONALD *does another movement. The same but slapping his ears.*

MAURICE. Er –

RONALD. Intense loneliness in a room in North London.

MAURICE. Thank you.

RONALD. What's this?

Entirely different and incomprehensible mime.

MAURICE. I don't know.

RONALD. An oil rig.

Awkward moment.

MAURICE. Lovely.

RONALD. Thank you.

MAURICE. And so it was –

RONALD. Ah yes! And so it was Joseph the son of Joseph and Mary the son of – Mary was betrothed and then married. To each other.

MAURICE. Obviously.

RONALD. Obviously. They had a big Greek Wedding in the local –

MAURICE. Jewish Wedding!

RONALD. Jewish Wedding in the local tearoom and the whole village come to the huge celebration they done but then, after the first flush of excitement, life become swiftly humdrum as it done before.

   RONALD *positions the chair.* RONALD *puts on his veil. Sits.*

   SFX: Mid-Eastern village.

Nazareth – Mary and Joseph's kitchen

Enter MAURICE *as* JOSEPH.

MARY. You're late, Joseph!

JOSEPH. What do you mean I'm late?

MARY. Where have you been?

JOSEPH. I've been working, haven't I?

MARY. I don't know what you've been doing.

JOSEPH. I've been building a patio.

MARY. I don't know what you been up to!

JOSEPH. Every day we go through this!

MARY. So? You don't know! You've got no bloody idea what it's like! Stuck here on my own!

JOSEPH. You've got the temple-mending.

MARY. Sodding temple-mending! Do you know what it's like hemming veils all day long? I'm going mad here!

JOSEPH. Well, you should get out more. Go swimming. Go to the – pictures. Go and see Elizabeth and Zachariah.

MARY. Elizabeth and Zachariah! I got nothing to say to Elizabeth and Zachariah!

JOSEPH. She's having a baby, isn't she?

MARY. So?

JOSEPH. She's having John the Baptist, isn't she?

MARY. Yes, and doesn't she just know it! Anyway, they're always reading. I'm young! I'm a young vibrant girl! I've got a whole life ahead of me. I *had* a whole life ahead of me. You want me stuck here, don't you. So you know exactly where I am. So you can keep your tabs on me!

JOSEPH. You don't have to stay!

MARY. Oh thank you very much. The minute I start complaining you want me out! Well maybe I will! Maybe I'll just leave!

JOSEPH. Or better still – I'll leave!

MARY. Alright! You leave!

JOSEPH. Alright I will! Goodbye!

MARY. Goodbye!

JOSEPH. Goodbye!

MARY. GOODBYE!

JOSEPH *slams the invisible door.* MARY *bursts into tears.*
MAURICE *becomes the* ARCHANGEL GABRIEL. *He
'flies' in round the stage and circles* MARY *who still sobs
bitterly.* GABRIEL *ascends* MRS F's *chair. He stands,
flapping his wings and speaks sonorously.*

GABRIEL. Mary? Mary? Mary –

RONALD *stops sobbing, steps forward.*

RONALD. Erm – ladies and gentlemen – due to the fact that
I been – cast in this production as Mary *and* Gabriel, it is
obviously not possible for me – to appear – unto my – self –

MAURICE – *stuck on* MRS F's *chair – has to listen as*
RONALD *goes on.*

– except perhaps in those higher states of mystic transport to
what I have not, as yet, attained. That being so, and taking
into account the ephemeral and ethereal nature of the angelic
species, on top of which few of us here have actually ever
actually seen an angel, Maurice will now appear to Mary as
the Archangel Gabriel and I shall later resume his cosmic
mantle later. Thank you.

He becomes MARY *and sits on the chair again. He puts
on his veil. Continues sobbing.* MAURICE *whooshes his
wings again.*

GABRIEL. Mary? Mary? Mary?

MARY. What? What? What?

GABRIEL. Are you alone?

MARY. Yes.

GABRIEL. Entirely alone?

MARY. Yes. Apart from the cat.

MAURICE. What?

MARY. Apart from the cat.

RONALD *has just put this in.*

MAURICE. What do you mean the cat?

MARY. Well, it's a black pussy with little white socks and pointy ears.

MAURICE. Yes I know what a cat is, Ronald.

RONALD. I put it in.

MAURICE. So is it going to become a regular feature then, is it, this cat, is it?

RONALD. Well, I thought it'd give a domestic element to the scene that would juxtapose nicely with the transcendental quality of the angel.

MAURICE. Did you?

RONALD. Yes.

MAURICE. Well, I want it out.

RONALD. You want it out?

MAURICE. Yes please.

RONALD. Come on then, puss. Puss! Puss! Come on, out! *OUT!*

He kicks the cat out. The cat runs back. He catches it. Chucks it out.

MAURICE. Thank you.

He sighs. Whooshes his wings again. Resumes the scene.

GABRIEL. Entirely alone?

MARY. Yes.

GABRIEL. Are you afraid?

MARY. No. Well a bit. Yes. Why?

GABRIEL. Blessed are you above all women. And all men.

MARY. Am I?

GABRIEL. Yes.

MARY. Why?

GABRIEL. Cos you shall conceive a son.

MARY. I'm only fourteen.

GABRIEL. You shall bring him forth in the dead of night. In the midst of winter shall you bring forth he. And you shall call his name Wonderful, Marvellous, Peace-Maker, Councillor, Beautiful, Magical, Fabulous, Triffic, Brill, and you will love him.

MARY. Will I?

GABRIEL. Yes!

MARY. But I haven't got it in me.

GABRIEL (*alarmed*). How do you mean!!?

MARY. No nothing. I will. I will love him. I'll – try.

GABRIEL. Course you will. You will be alright.

MARY. Will I?

GABRIEL. Yes!

MARY. Right.

GABRIEL. And no strong drink shall he –

MRS FFLYTE *enters. She marches through the back tabs, graciously acknowledging applause. She knows she's late but she's ignoring it. She stops when she sees* MAURICE *is on her chair.* RONALD *looks at* MAURICE. *An awkward moment.* MRS F *whispers to* RONALD. RONALD *nips over.*

RONALD. Are you alright, Mrs F?

MRS F *whispers.*

(*Leans closer.*) Sorry?

MRS F *whispers louder, points at her chair.*

MAURICE. And no strong drink shall he –

RONALD *runs back to* MAURICE.

RONALD. *She wants her chair!*

MAURICE. *I'm on the chair. I'm doin' the speech! She's on too soon. Get her off!*

And no strong drink shall he –

MRS F (*hisses*). *Ronald!!!*

> RONALD *agonised as he looks from* MAURICE *to* MRS F.
> *He is caught between two chairs. At last, he takes* MARY*'s*
> *chair. Brings it to* MAURICE. *Puts it beside the plush chair.*

MAURICE. *Ronald!!! What the hell you playin' at?!*

RONALD. *I can't do nothing about it!*

> MAURICE *steps off* MRS F*'s chair. Gets on the kitchen*
> *chair.* MRS F *sits on her chair, satisfied.* MAURICE
> *whooshes his wings, wobbles. Continues as* GABRIEL.

GABRIEL. And – no strong drink shall he drink. And he shall
not smoke. And no razor shall he put to his head. And he
shall be an vegetarian. Or possibly vegan, depending on the
availability of local foodstuffs.

MARY. We're not getting on. I know it's my fault. But we'd be
terrible parents.

> MRS F *rises majestically, about to sing.*

GABRIEL. NO –

> MRS F *sits.*

– without a man shall ye conceive! Whist a virgin shall ye
bring forth, whilst a virgin shall ye give suck. For the power
of the Most High shall be upon thee without any of the heat
of lust!

MARY. I'm scared now.

GABRIEL. There is no need for fear. The seed is planted. He is
there already.

> MRS F *rises. Now is the right time.*

Song 1: Handel, 'Comfort Ye My People'

MRS F (*sings*).
  Comfort ye.

GABRIEL. In the twinkling of an eye.

MRS F (*sings*).
Comfort ye my people.
Saith your God.
Saith your God.
Speak ye comfortably to Jerusalem.
Speak ye comfortably to Jerusalem.
And cry unto her
That her warfare is accomplished
That her iniquity is pardoned
That her iniquity is pardoned.

MAURICE and RONALD *move.* MRS F *has not finished.*

The voice of him –

MAURICE and RONALD *freeze.*

– that crieth in the wilderness –

MAURICE leans towards her.

MAURICE (*whispers*). Mrs F –

MRS F (*sings*).
– prepare ye the way of the Lord.

MAURICE. Mrs F –

MRS F (*sings*).
Make straight in the desert a highway –

MAURICE (*more urgent*). Mrs F!?

MRS F (*sings*).
– for our Go-od!!!

MRS F *sees* MAURICE. *Jumps.*

MAURICE. Thank you so much.

MRS F. Thank you.

She sits back in her chair. MAURICE *crosses the stage to be* JOSEPH *again.*

RONALD. That following evening, Joseph was working in his workshop –

MAURICE *mimes hammering a nail.*

– drumming. When all of a sudden the Archangel Gabriel appeared again.

He stops, walks towards the front.

Um – although in this scene I shall be playin' Gabriel due to the fact that Mary who I will be still be will be still be playing later does not appear till –

MAURICE. I think they've got the point now, Ronald.

RONALD. Have they?

MAURICE. Yes.

RONALD. Thank you!

> RONALD *turns his back. He begins to whistle strangely.*
> MAURICE *is* JOSEPH *again.*

Nazareth – Joseph's workshop

JOSEPH. Hello? Who's that!? Who's there? Hello? Mary?

> RONALD *turns as* GABRIEL. *He lifts his arms as wings.*

GABRIEL. Joseph?

JOSEPH. Yes?

GABRIEL. Mary's going to have a baby.

JOSEPH. Sorry?

GABRIEL. Mary's going to have a baby.

JOSEPH. How? We haven't –

GABRIEL. It is a miracle. Do not question it.

JOSEPH. No. Right.

GABRIEL. She's having a baby.

JOSEPH. She's having a baby?

GABRIEL. She's having a baby.

JOSEPH. So – um – do you need me to – er –

GABRIEL. No.

JOSEPH. And it's not – mine?

GABRIEL. No.

JOSEPH. No. So is it anybody I –

GABRIEL. No.

JOSEPH. No.

GABRIEL. It is the Holy Spirit.

> JOSEPH *gasps*.

> He entered her womb on a shaft of light. It will be an holy birth.

JOSEPH (*taking this in*). Holy birth. Right. Yes. Um gottit. And you're – an angel?

GABRIEL. I'm an archangel!

JOSEPH. Sorry.

GABRIEL. Got the picture now?

JOSEPH. Yes thank you. So – um – when's it due?

GABRIEL. Christmas.

JOSEPH. Right.

GABRIEL. If that's alright with you.

JOSEPH. Fine yes. We was thinking of going away but –

GABRIEL. You will be going away.

JOSEPH. Where?

GABRIEL. It will be – um – (*Hasn't been told.*) revealed.

> JOSEPH *looks up at* GABRIEL.

JOSEPH. Why – um – us?

GABRIEL. You are beloved.

JOSEPH. Sorry?

GABRIEL. You are beloved! (*Puts his wing around* JOSEPH.)

JOSEPH. You should see us, though. We're never happy. We're always arguing. Even talking about div–

GABRIEL. *You are beloved!!!*

JOSEPH. Right.

> GABRIEL *flaps his wings, jumps off the chair and lands heavily. Then whooshes out to the side of the stage.*

GABRIEL. Geddit?

JOSEPH. Yes thank you.

> GABRIEL *whooshes. Exits.*
>
> MAURICE *walks between the pillars.*
>
> *SFX: Crickets, night-time sounds.*

Nazareth – Mary's room

RONALD *enters. He is* MARY. *He sits nervously on the seat. Puts on veil.* MAURICE *is* JOSEPH *again. He walks up quietly behind her.*

JOSEPH. Mary?

MARY. Yes, Joseph?

JOSEPH. Um –

MARY. What?

JOSEPH. I know about the baby.

MARY. Don't know what you're talking about.

JOSEPH. I heard it in a dream.

MARY. Did you?

JOSEPH. Yes.

MARY. I was going to tell you, I promise.

JOSEPH. Mary –

MARY. Did you have an angel?

JOSEPH. An *arch*angel.

MARY. Oh.

JOSEPH. Mary –

MARY. I don't know what's happening, Joseph! I don't know what I done!

JOSEPH. I just want to say –

MARY. You going to cast me out then?

JOSEPH. – I will stay with you. Even when the night is at its blackest. Even unto the brink will I stick with you. Even unto the dark cave in the frozen grip of winter. Even unto death will I be with you.

MARY. Thank you very much.

JOSEPH. So – d'you want anything at all – any er – Horlicks? Anything like that?

MARY. No thank you.

JOSEPH. It is a miracle, Mary.

MARY. Is it?

JOSEPH. I believe so, yes.

MARY. Right.

JOSEPH. What are you thinking?

MARY. I'm pondering.

JOSEPH. In your heart?

MARY. Yes.

MRS F *starts to sing. This takes them by surprise. They both turn to her.*

Song 2: Handel, 'Behold I Tell you a Mystery'

MRS F (*sings*).

Behold – I tell you a mystery. We shall not all sleep but we shall all be changed in a moment in the twinkling of an eye. At the last trumpet!

MAURICE. Exactly.

They all exit.

Music (orchestral): 'Veni Veni Emmanuel'. Dramatic lighting change.

Desert

RONALD *enters in turban and flowing robes. He mimes riding a camel. He is the* FIRST WISE MAN. *Next* MAURICE *enters, also in robes and turban. He also mimes riding a camel. He is the* SECOND WISE MAN. *They stop, sense each other's presence, see each other and wave. Now* MRS F *enters, also in turban and robe and on a camel. She rides past till she too senses the others' presence. She turns and they all wave to each other. At that moment the* HOLY STAR *appears. They all GASP. They start to gallop after the star. The star turns and reverses.* MAURICE's WISE MAN *does not notice and continues to ride on.* RONALD *and* MRS F's WISE MEN *see the star turn. They try to tell* MAURICE *but he has gone. They realise there is nothing else for it but to follow the star in its reverse direction. They follow the star and exit. A moment later,* MAURICE *reappears. He follows the star alone across the stage.* RONALD *reappears from the wing, points to the star.* MAURICE *rides past him. Exits.*

Music ends.

Stage – general

RONALD. Thank you. Thank you very much. And now where
was we? Ah yes. So let us now pick up the story once –
again where we was – left off.

MAURICE (*off*). Where we left off.

RONALD. Was left off.

MAURICE (*off*). Where we left off!

RONALD. I said that! And so it come to pass in them days that
word went out unto Caesar Augustus that rebellion and
mutiny was in the air and the people was all amurmurin' in
discontentnentment. So Caesar didst decree a new decree
that all the world should be counted. So he would know
exactly were they was and what they was up to and so he
could nip any rebellion in the bud before it happened. And so
didst he ordained that all the people should go without delay
unto his or her own city where they was born and do – the
Roman Census.

Music: fanfare.

MAURICE *enters in a Roman breast plate and helmet.*

MAURICE. Thank you. And now –

Music: fanfare.

Thank you. And now –

RONALD. Very nice, Maurice.

MAURICE. Thank you. And now –

RONALD. Very fetching.

MAURICE. Thank you. And now, ladies and gentlemen, let us
step back in time back to those misty days of yesteryear as
we present an – historically authenticated re-enactment of
the Roman Census – as it almost certainly would have been,
would have been. So, in order to facilitate this historic event
in all its full and historic authenticity, we will ask you
yourselves to assume the role of the jostling and noisome
populace thronging the darkened alleyways and garish souks

of the Nazareth Civic Centre. For this uniquely researched sequence, I myself will play the elegant but heartless Roman Tribune Lucius Maximus Asparagus who has arrived from Rome to conduct the hated Roman Census.

Puts on helmet. RONALD *stares at it.*

And, Ronald –

RONALD. Nice shiny helmet, Maurice.

MAURICE. Thank you. And Ronald will be taking the role of the Mayor of Nazareth, a self-taught political activist and rabble-rouser.

RONALD *puts on his little mayor hat. Ties under his chin.*

Welding the crowd into a fervid hotbed of rebellious rage.

RONALD *waves.*

Which he will be doin' whilst I will utter certain hated words that fire in you the spark of seething passion. So – whenever you hear the word 'Rome' you murmur and mutter in a discontented manner. Whenever you hear the word 'Caesar' you go: 'HAH!' And whenever you hear the word 'Census' fall from my hated lips, you shout: 'What do you think we are, a statistic?' Right got that? Good. Let's just take that out for a spin. Shall we?

Audience practice.

I didn't quite hear that! Where's all the rebellious spirit I heard so much about?

Audience practice.

Already it has reached the the ears of Caesar in Rome as he plans the Census!

Audience practice.

Ah yes! Marvellous and highly authentic. So authentic, in fact, it was almost as if we was actually there. Finally, if you are fortunate enough to receive one of our numbered and hand-embossed 'character cards'.

RONALD *displays character cards.*

Thank you, Ronald. Now please await the calling of your number before attempting to utter these historically authenticated phrases written thereon that will be skillfully interwoven by the Mayor into the fabric of the Tribune's speech that will be delivered, of course, by myself. So now we present the Roman Census as it might almost certainly have been. Thank you.

RONALD. But lo! Look, citizens! The hated Tribune! On his hated –

MAURICE. I've got to leave the stage first, Ronald!

MAURICE *exits.*

Music: fanfare.

MAURICE *marches back on.*

Music continues.

RONALD. But lo! Look, citizens! The hated Tribune! On his hated horse!

MAURICE. I'm walking, Ronald!

RONALD. What?

MAURICE. I'm on foot.

RONALD. On his hated foot!

MAURICE *cuts music. It stops abruptly.*

MAURICE. Oh, Nazarenes! I have come from Rome. I said I have come from ROME!

Audience murmur and mutter.

Sent by CAESAR.

Audience: 'Hah!'

To conduct the Roman CENSUS!

Audience: 'What do you think we are, a statistic?'

So if you wouldn't mind forming an orderly –

RONALD. Number One please!

NUMBER ONE. Bugger off!

MAURICE. So if you wouldn't mind –

RONALD. Number Two please –

NUMBER TWO. Call that a six-pack!

MAURICE. – wouldn't mind –

RONALD. Number Three!

NUMBER THREE. Cornetto, please!

MAURICE. – just forming a –

RONALD. Number Four!

NUMBER FOUR. Wot! No Referendum!

MAURICE (*exasperated*). – forming a queue –

RONALD. Number Five please.

NUMBER FIVE. Up your Appian way!

MAURICE. – in an orderly manner –

RONALD. Number Six please!

NUMBER SIX. Toss yourself off in the Tiber!

RONALD. Number Seven please!

NUMBER SEVEN. Get back to Rome!

Audience murmur and mutter.

MAURICE. – orderly –

RONALD. Number Eight!

NUMBER EIGHT. Stuff Caesar!

Audience: 'Hah!'

MAURICE. – orderly –

RONALD. Number Nine!

NUMBER NINE. Stick it up your Census!

Audience: 'What do you think we are, a statistic?'

MAURICE. – orderly queue –

RONALD. Number Ten please!

MAURICE. Ronald?

RONALD. Number Eleven!

MAURICE. *Ronald!*

RONALD. Number –

MAURICE. Ronald!!!

RONALD. Number –

MAURICE. RONALD!!

RONALD. What?

MAURICE. What are you doing?

RONALD. Welding the crowd into a fervid hotbed of rebellious rage, oh hated Tribune.

MAURICE. The historically authenticated phrases, Ronald, were supposed to be interwoven into the delicate fabric of the Census –

RONALD. What do you think we are, a statistic!!!?

MAURICE. Ronald, I'm trying to begin the Census –

RONALD. What do you think we are –

MAURICE. I'm doin' the Census!!!!

RONALD. WHAT DO YOU THINK WE ARE –

MAURICE. RONALD!! If I can't have your cooperation on this – I'm going to have to cut it.

RONALD. Cut what?

MAURICE. The Census!

RONALD *and* AUDIENCE. WHAT DO YOU THINK WE ARE, A –

MAURICE (*to whole audience*). Will you shut up!!! You're just encouraging him! You've got him hopelessly overexcited now! I mean look at him!

RONALD *looks embarrassed*.

Cap off, Ronald!

RONALD. You fuck off.

MAURICE. CAP off, Ronald!!!

RONALD. Right.

Pulls his cap off.

MAURICE. I now see there is a small but dangerous minority amongst you here tonight who are using Ronald as a tool. To further your own subversive ends. You're being used, Ronald!

RONALD. Sorry.

MAURICE. Right. We'll carry on now.

RONALD. Number Seventeen!!

MAURICE. No no no! We've cut the Census!

AUDIENCE *and* RONALD. WHAT DO YOU THINK WE ARE, A –

MAURICE. All right. That's it! THAT IS IT!!!!! Because of the pathetic and puerile behaviour of certain individuals here this evening, there will be no more audience participation for the rest of the performance! And I hope that those I am referring to, and they know precisely who they are, are quite satisfied now that they've spoilt everybody else's fun. And now, ladies and gentlemen, there will now be a brief interval or intermission. During which time I would ask you to blackball all the troublemakers in the audience and do NOT – however much they plead – succumb to buying them any drinks, peanuts or porky scratchings. In fact, simply ignore them. It's the only way they'll learn. The rest of you, please avail yourselves of the delightful attractive culinary facilities in the delightful catering areas on all levels, where a wide selection of bar snacks, light refreshments, alcoholic beverages, hot and cold drinks and squashes are being served. Also – why not pay a visit our uniquely themed 'Gift Shop' where a whole heavenly host of attractive souvenirs, memorabilia and stocking-fillers are on sale, including donkey pencil-sharpeners, humorous halos, wise-men flip-flops, angel coasters and frozen organic shepherd's pies. Thank you.

Music.

They march through the back drapes. Get jammed between two pillars. Exit with difficulty.

End of Act One.

ACT TWO

Music: Overture.

Stage – general

Enter MAURICE *and* RONALD. RONALD *signals offstage. Same as Act One.*

Music cuts.

MAURICE. And now, ladies and gentlemen – Ronald and myself take great pleasure in commencing our second act – or 'Act Two' – by presenting – in person – our special guest star here tonight, as we was hopin' to do at the commentcement of our afore-performed 'Act One'. Ladies and gentlemen – Mrs Leonora Fflyte.

Music: fanfare.

Enter MRS F.

MRS F. Thank you, thank you.

MAURICE. Thank you.

RONALD. Thank you.

MAURICE. Thank you. Her illustrious career has seen her doin' the singin' in many famous opera houses and many other – houses also. Playin' the fulmost gamut of mighty operatic roles, includin' Carmen, Tosca, Brunhilde, Rigoletto, The Merry Widow, Widow Twanky. But now it is now our great privilege to invite –

RONALD. Mrs F –

MAURICE. Mrs F to lead the company in one of the loveliest arias –

MRS F. It's not an aria.

RONALD. He doesn't know his arias from his elbow, Mrs F.

MAURICE. – ever penned by our musical inspiration for our show here tonight – Johann Sebastian Handel.

MRS F. 'For Unto Us a Child is Born'! Which shall be sung algusto vivace tutti.

RONALD. Wh'she sayin?

MAURICE. I have no idea.

MAURICE and RONALD exit.

MRS F. Two and three and –

Song 3: Handel, 'For Unto Us a Child is Born'

For unto us a child is born –

MAURICE and RONALD dance in and sing beside her.

ALL.
Unto us, a child is born, unto us a son is given – (*Etc.*)

And the government shall be upon His shoulder; and his name shall be called Wonderful Counsellor, the Mighty God, the Everlasting Father, the Prince of Peace. The Everlasting Father, the Prince of Peace. The Everlasting Father, the Prince of Peace.

They bow. MRS F takes the applause. She bows and curtsies.

Curtsies. MAURICE bows. RONALD curtsies. MAURICE and RONALD exit. MRS F takes centre-stage.

MRS F. And so it was Joseph setteth Mary upon the donkey and verily didst they travel through many days and many nights unto Bethlehem.

MRS F returns to her chair.

Music: Road to Bethlehem.

Enter MARY sitting on the imaginary donkey. JOSEPH leading her. They travel across the stage. MRS F watches from her chair.

JOSEPH. Are you alright, Mary? On the donkey?

MARY. I'm okay.

JOSEPH. Comfy?

MARY. The baby's kicking a bit.

JOSEPH. Another precipitous hairpin coming up, sorry.

They manoeuvre the hairpin. MARY *hangs on.*

Don't look down!

MARY (*looks over a cliff*). Oh!

JOSEPH. Alright?

MARY. Is it much further?

JOSEPH. Erm – a little bit further yes.

MARY. How much further?

JOSEPH. Sorry?

MARY. How much further?

JOSEPH. Would you like a little rest now?

MARY. How much further?!

JOSEPH. Three hundred and ninety-one miles.

MARY. Three hun– oh no! I can't stand it. It's been miles and miles and miles!

JOSEPH. We'll have a little rest now.

MARY. Take me down from the donkey, Joseph!

JOSEPH *pulls up the donkey, helps* MARY *down.*

Be careful!

JOSEPH. I am being careful.

JOSEPH *leads the donkey to a member of the audience.*

Excuse me. Will you hold the donkey please? Thank you.

MARY. He's called Parsley. You can stroke him if you want. Not there.

(*Sighs.*) I got to have a sit-down, Joseph! I'm exhausted!

JOSEPH. Look! How about in this nice little tiny little dark cave I just found?

MARY (*suddenly* RONALD). Don't want to go in a nice little tiny little dark cave!

JOSEPH (*improvising*). Do not be – um – afeared, Mary, mine wife.

RONALD. Don't want to go in the little tiny little dark cave!

MAURICE. Alright alright! It's not a real cave, is it? It's only actin', Ronald! (*Laughs to audience.*)

RONALD (*panicking, sotto*). You know I don't like it, Maurice! I don't like it, I don't like it!

MAURICE/JOSEPH. Alright alright! Then – then – how about – *in front* of the nice little dark tiny little dark cave? Just here?

MARY. Alright. Help me sit down then please.

JOSEPH. Alright?

MARY. Yes thank you.

JOSEPH *helps* MARY *sit.*

JOSEPH. Shall I make a little fire now?

MARY. Are you up to making a little fire?

JOSEPH. Yes I am up to making a little fire. Actually. For lo, the angel said –

MARY. I know what the angel said. He appeared to me too you know!

JOSEPH. I know he appeared to you too!

JOSEPH *starts collecting firewood. He arranges sticks for a fire.*

MARY. There's no use repeating everything I say. Whatchoo doin'?

JOSEPH. Collectin' kindlin'.

MARY. Where's the angel now, that's what I want to know? It's all very well him coming and telling us things, but when the going gets tough he's nowhere to be seen.

JOSEPH. He's probably watching over us or something I should imagine.

Starts rubbing flints.

MARY. Winging about. Having a nice time in the clouds, more likely. What are we going to do, Joseph! What are we going to do in Bethlehem?

JOSEPH *battling with the flints.*

Have you thought of that? Where are we going to stay? Where am I going to lay my poor weary head, Joseph? Do they know I'm pregnant? Have you booked? Did you get en suite? What's going to happen, Joseph!? What are we going to do!? *Joseph! Joseph!!!*

JOSEPH. No!!!! I haven't booked alright!? I don't know what we're goin to do! Don't know where we're going to stay! I don't know what's going to happen! I don't know what en suite is! I don't know what all this is about! I'm just trying to do my best. Alright!??

Painful moment.

MARY. I'm sorry, Joseph. It's just I get so tired on that donkey.

They gaze at the donkey, still being held by the audience member.

Alright, Parsley? Mind he doesn't munch your jumper.

(*Back to* JOSEPH.) I don't mean to nag, Joseph.

JOSEPH. That's alright, Mary.

He rubs the flints again. At last, a flame. He lights the sticks. The fire lights. Glows red on their faces. They gaze into the fire.

MARY. It's a nice little fire.

JOSEPH. Yes. Shall we turn in now?

MARY. Alright.

They lie down.

Goodnight, Joseph.

JOSEPH. Goodnight, Mary.

MARY. Goodnight.

JOSEPH. Goodnight.

MARY. Goodnight, Mrs F.

MRS F surprised. Nods back. They all close their eyes.

MAURICE. The tiny fire flickered in the cold night air.

The fire flickers.

And then it went out.

The fire goes out. MARY wakes with a start.

MARY. Joseph!!! The fire's gone out. Joseph! I can't see. There are no shapes in the darkness. There are no stars in the sky. Joseph! I'm cold. I can't see. Joseph! Joseph! Joseph!!! Joseph!!!!

JOSEPH (*wakes, jumps up*). Alright, alright, alright!

He blows the spark. Slowly the fire lights again.

There.

They gaze at the fire.

MARY. Hold me.

Tentatively JOSEPH puts his arm round MARY. The light of the fire glows on their faces.

I don't understand. I don't know what's going on.

JOSEPH. No.

MARY. Do you know what's going on?

JOSEPH. No. It is a mystery. I'll watch the fire. You sleep now.

MARY. Alright.

> *She remembers Parsley.*

> (*Calls.*) Parsley?

> *They mime Parsley rejoining them.* MARY *sleeps.*

Above Bethlehem

MRS F *stands. She sings.*

Song 4: Handel, 'Come Unto Him All Ye That Labour'

As she sings, MAURICE *stands. He discreetly crosses the stage and through the back drapes, leaving* RONALD *alone as the sleeping* MARY.

Slowly the back drapes open. We see revealed a perfect little Christmas-card Bethlehem. Little houses, little lights in the little windows. The drapes continue being drawn, accidentally revealing MAURICE *proudly winding the handle, marvelling at his creation. He notices the audience and sharply winds the drapes back a bit. He returns to* RONALD, *still asleep as* MARY. *Remembers something and nips back behind the drapes. A stable trundles on, halts next to the town. A little donkey beside the stable.* MAURICE *runs back to* RONALD *again. Kneels beside him. Remembers again. He gets up again. Each time he gets up,* RONALD *lolls.* MAURICE *leans into the stable and pull a switch. A little light shines in the stable window. He climbs out of the model town and accidentally knocks over a tower. He tries to set it right. It falls again. He tries again. It falls again. He noisily shoves it back into place. Runs back to his position next to* RONALD. *He puts his arm round* MARY. MRS F *finishes the aria.*

RONALD (*whispering*). Are you playing games or sommink?

MAURICE. What?

RONALD. Hoppin' up and down like a bloody great toad!

MAURICE. Bloody great what?

RONALD. Toad! Leaving me all alone in that scene, pregnant and unattended. Like a lemon! Fiddlin' about with your cardboard houses!

MAURICE. I was only thinking of you and Mrs F, Ronald!

RONALD. You was only thinkin' of yourself! You and your clever-clogs special effects!

MAURICE. I was merely attempting to enhance and preserve the theatrical moment, as it happens, Ronald.

RONALD. So some stinkin' little cardboard town is more important to you than a woman in her most vulnerable moment, about to give birth in the middle of the Syrian desert. Do you have any idea what a difficult time I've had attempting this role? Have you ever tried playing a fourteen-year-old virgin?

MAURICE. I happen to think it has stretched you enormously, Ronald.

RONALD. I don't give a fig for what you think, Maurice! Neither does Mrs F, if you want to know!

MRS F *freezes*.

Cos we've been discussing you in the dressing room and we both agree it's just 'self self self' with you!

MAURICE. Really?

RONALD. Yes.

MAURICE. Well – in that case – I suggest we stop the show right here and now and put our cards on the table. Say exactly what we all feel. Mrs F? Would you like to begin? Anything you'd like to – er – 'share' with everybody here?

MRS F *is horrified*.

RONALD. Oh, here we go! You and your bloody psycho drama-therapy sessions. 'Oh hello welcome to the group. And who'd like to speak first?' 'Actually I'm going to speak first! For the next five bloody hours!'

MAURICE. Just exactly where is this conversation leading, may I ask?!

RONALD. You're a hypocrite!

MAURICE. Oh really!?

RONALD. And a superfluous hypocrite at that!

MRS F. Superficial.

RONALD. Superferlatial hypocrite at that! 'Oh look everyone! I just decided I become a "vegan". I can't have no milk or eggs in my tea. Oh but wait a minute! Oh no! Actually on second thoughts. I will have a third helpin' of puddin' please! And another couple dollops of custard! Vegan custard? Nah! Full-fat!' We're not surprised she left you. Are we, Mrs F? Mrs F? Don't know how she lived with you. If you want to know. That – that – Morag!

MAURICE. Maureen.

RONALD. Morgan.

MAURICE. Maureen!

RONALD. Maureen!! Not surprised she left you.

MAURICE. So now you've had your say, Ronald, now you've expressed your feelin's about me, what would you suggest I do now, Ronald ?

RONALD. I do suggest you go back to showin' ladies Hoover parts at Debenhams.

Shocked moment. No one speaks.

Right. I am goin' off now.

RONALD *exits. Then re-enters.*

Then I'm coming back on as Herod.

Exits again.

MAURICE. RONALD!

RONALD *re-enters.*

RONALD. Yes?

MAURICE. I will fulfil my contractual agreement with you with regardin' tonight's show, Ronald. After that – as far as I'm concerned – this partnership is OVER!

RONALD. And I shall be doin' Herod with the nose!

Marches off and exits. MAURICE *shouts into wing.*

MAURICE. Alright, Ronald! If you want to play it like that!

MAURICE *has no option but to exit too.* MRS F *remains mortified, glued to her seat.*

SFX: Thunder and lightning.

Music.

Jerusalem – Herod's palace

RONALD *enters in cape and crown. He turns dramatically. He is wearing a long nose.*

HEROD. Aha! I am Herod the King. Otherwise known as King Herod. Sorry to have kept you. I just been out persecuting my people! Ha ha ha ha ha!!!

MAURICE *re-enters in a* WISE MAN *hat and costume.*

Aha! But who do we have we here? No, no, don't tell me. You must be – the Three Wise Men I've heard so much about.

WISE MAN (*forced into it*). We, er, are yes. And we have news to impart unto thee!

HEROD. News to umpart into me?

WISE MAN. Yes! We have seen a new star, Your Highness. A-shinin' in the night. And we have followed it.

HEROD. A NEW STAR did you say? A-shinin' in the night?

WISE MAN. Yes.

HEROD. So where is it now, this NEW STAR?

WISE MAN. Above your palace, Your Highness.

HEROD. Above my palace?! Let me see!

WISE MAN. Just up there, Your Highness.

He points to the right. The giant star tracks in very fast from the left. Jerks to a stop. WISE MAN *points to the left.* HEROD *gasps.*

HEROD. Ah yes! So it is! Could it be – a portent?

WISE MAN. Yes, O Herod! We believe it could be!

HEROD. An important portent?

WISE MAN. Yes! A most important portent!

HEROD. So what could it portend, this most important portent?

WISE MAN. What could it portend, this most important portent?

HEROD. Yes.

WISE MAN. Well we believe –

HEROD. Yes?

WISE MAN. – it could portend –

HEROD. Right?

WISE MAN. – could portend –

HEORD. Yes?

WISE MAN. Don't keep doin' that.

HEROD. Right.

WISE MAN. The arrival of a great king!

HEROD. Arrival of a great – but that's me, isn't it?! I'm the great king! The greatest king OF ALL! There is no greater king!!! No GREATER KING THAN ME!!!

HEROD leaps up and down like a wild toddler.

WISE MAN. Are you alright, Your Highness?

HEROD. Yes, thank you.

Dramatically calms down.

Tell you what! I'll just – nip down my catacombs to see if I can find any relevant info. Won't keep you.

Turns.

Would you like anything? Sherry?

WISE MAN. No thank you.

HEROD. Twiglets?

WISE MAN. I'm vegetarian.

HEROD. It's only Marmite.

MAURICE. And so it was Herod went straightway unto his secret catacombs which he done under his palace. First through a mighty door he went.

HEROD *mimes opening a mighty door.*

SFX: Creaking door.

Music.

Then by the light of flickering candlelight down along a long long long passageway.

HEROD *creeps along a passageway.*

Till he came to a flight of steps. Down the steps he went.

HEROD *goes down many steps.*

Down and down. Down and down.

Down more steps.

Through a tiny opening in the damp cold wall –

Through a tiny opening.

– and on down into the Chinese puzzle of more and more dark dark corridors, growing ever darker and darker.

Down dark dark corridors.

Until at last – he came – to a mighty door. Hewn of gopher wood!

A mighty door. He slowly wrenches it open.

SFX: Door creaks.

He stepped inside and saw before him a tiny little dark little room.

He is in a tiny room. He gasps!

At last he found what he was looking for. It was the Room of Prophecies!! Feverishly his hand flicked across a multitude of little tiny volumes. All the prophecies ever prophesied!

HEROD*'s hand flicks across a multitude of tiny imagined scrolls. He peers at the titles, one by one.*

The Plagues of Egypt, Belshazzar's Feast, Pharaoh's Dream, the Revelation of St John the Divine, the Foretelling of the Birth –

Gasps!

– of the *MESSIAH*!

He snatches a tiny scroll. Unrolls it feverishly. Reads aloud.

HEROD. For lo – the people who doth walk in the darkness will see a great light and the great light will be a great king, a new king, and the new king will be a little baby and the little baby will be the Messiah. And he will be born in the little town of Bethlehem!

Looks up.

SHIT!

MAURICE. And then just at that moment, the mighty door of gopher wood slammed behind him. BOOM! The single candle went out. FIZZZ! The tiny coffin-like Room of Prophecies was plunged into darkness. And Herod found himself incarcerated in a living tomb! Fifty foot below the palace!!! There was no escape! The walls, floor and ceiling started to close in on Ronald. Herod!

RONALD *begins to panic.*

RONALD. I don't like it, Maurice!

MAURICE. Embracing him in a deathly vice-like grip. From which there was no escape!

RONALD (*panicking more*). Can we stop now please!?

MAURICE. The darkness was all-consuming! The oxygen levels were critically low!

RONALD. Stop it, Maurice! You know I don't like it! I want to get out! Wanna get out!

MAURICE. Ronald!

RONALD. I'm goin' to be sick!

MAURICE. *Ronald!!*

RONALD. I don't like it, Maurice! I don't like the actin'.

RONALD *runs through the pillars and off the revolve then off the stage.* MAURICE *chases him.*

MAURICE. Ronald!!!

RONALD *runs through the auditorium. He charges through the stalls.* MAURICE *rushes after him shouting.*

Ronald!! What do you think Mrs F is thinking?

RONALD. I don't give an effin' eff what Mrs F is finking!

MAURICE. Ronald! Ronald! *Ronald!*

They rush out and exit.

We hear MAURICE *and* RONALD *shouting offstage, banging doors. Their voices trail away.* MRS F *realises she is all alone. She looks at the audience. Realises only she can save the show.*

MRS F. And now – (*Thinks.*) 'Musetta's Waltz Song' from *La bohème* by Puccini.

She stands and sings.

***Song 5: Puccini, 'Quando Me'n Vo' from* La bohème**

MRS F is soon consumed by the singing. RONALD, pursued by MAURICE, reappears in the auditorium. They rush back through the audience and jump back on the stage.
MAURICE chases RONALD. He tries to grab him.
RONALD avoids him. They leap over the model town.
RONALD crushes the stable. He grabs a pillar. Holds it threateningly.

MAURICE. Alright, Ronald! Put the pillar down! Give me the pillar, Ronald! Put it down, Ronald!

MAURICE gently takes the pillar. Puts it down. RONALD lurches dangerously towards the audience. MAURICE follows him. At last he grabs him.

Ronald! Ronald! I'm sorry! I'm sorry! I'm very very very sorry, Ronald! VERY VERY SORRY, RONALD!

At last RONALD goes still. MRS F sings on, totally immersed in Puccini. MAURICE tries to start the show again. Tries to shush MRS F who does not notice. She sings louder. MAURICE shushes her. She sings louder and louder. RONALD shouts out:

RONALD. *SHUT UP, MRS F!!!*

MAURICE looks at RONALD in shock. MRS F plonks, mortified, in her chair.

A dreadful silence.

MAURICE. So – um – Herod?

RONALD. Yes?

MAURICE. Did you find the – (*Puts on his* WISE MAN *hat.*) er, relevant info in the – er – catacombs?

RONALD. In the what?

MAURICE. Catacombs?

RONALD. CATACOMBS!!!

Snaps back into action.

YES!!! There does seem to be some sort of messianic figure prophesied.

Gasps.

A Messiah in Bethlehem!!!

WISE MAN. A Messiah!? In Bethlehem!?

HEROD. Messiah!!! In Bethlehem!!!! Messiah!!! In Bethlehem!!!

So look!! I tell you what!! (*Hyperventilating.*) Go straightway unto Bethlehem. And search ye diligently for him, for this tiny little baby, and when ye have found him, this – this – Messiah –

WISE MAN. Yes?

HEROD. – bring him straightway to me, that I may bow down unto him and worship him! Quick quick! Quick as you can, Wise Men! Bring him to ME! Hurry, Wise Men! Hurry hurry hurry!

WISE MAN (*bowing to* HEROD). Right. Certainly. Certainly! Yes, O King!

(*Whispering.*) Hurry hurry, Wise Men!! And collect our Wise Men's camels and leave this dark and wicked place. And find the tiny holy baby and warn the tiny holy parents to escape from Herod as fast as possible. Come, Wise Men, come! Come, Mrs –

Grabs MRS F *by the hand.*

– Wise Man – come! Goodbye, Your Highness. Goodbye!

They exit at speed.

SFX: Thunder clap and lighting.

Music.

HEROD (*waving after them*). Goodbye! Goodbyeee! Don't be lo-ong! Don't be –

He stops. Realises the truth.

Wait a minute!! Wait a MINUTE! Do they think I'm an idiot!? They're not going to find the baby! They're not going to bring him to me at all! They're going to WARN him about me and my horribly narcissistic psychopathic intentions! Ha! Quick!!! Send for my army! Tell 'em to get those old bastards! Those Wise Men! With all their peace and learnin' and wisdom and have 'em burned like torches in the street! Then when they done that, find every baby in the world and have 'em all – butchered! Stop those Wise Men! Find the baby!!! Find the baby!!!

SFX: Thunder clap and lighting.

Music.

HEROD *strides off laughing insanely.*

The revolve begins to spin with increasing speed. MAURICE *and* MRS F, *as* TWO WISE MEN, *enter. They jump on to the revolve. They whizz around, escaping from* HEROD, *searching for the baby.* RONALD *enters, still pulling on his* WISE MAN *outfit. He leaps for the revolve. The revolve goes faster. He falls off. He scrambles on, clutches a pillar, crashes into the others. They spin faster. They collapse on to each other. The revolve spins even faster. The three of them finish in a heap.*

Music: climaxes.

They stagger up. Look at each other.

RONALD. So shall we do the – er – Birth Scene now? Might get us er –

MAURICE. – back on track?

MRS F. Well, it is rather the point, isn't it?

RONALD. That's right, Mrs F? Isn't it, Maurice? Maurice?

MAURICE. Right.

MRS F. Robes!!

RONALD *and* MAURICE *are blank.*

ROBES!!

RONALD *and* MAURICE. ROBES!!!

They pull off their robes. RONALD *folds them up. Chucks them into the wing.* MRS F *returns to her chair.*

MAURICE. So do you want to do the er –

RONALD. Yes. Right. Thank you. So – now, ladies and gentlemen, we come to that bit of the show which is possibly the most difficult of all in that it requires us to perform what has never been performed on stage before. That is the birth of a baby as done by two men. Thank you.

MAURICE. We feel – Ronald and I feel – that it is important to make clear that this is in no way meant to be in any way insensitive or in bad taste. We could have omitted this scene obviously but – we felt it was –

RONALD. – crucial to the piece. In this scene I shall be playing the mother, Mary, via the aid of mimin' and also portraying Josephine the midwife. Whilst Maurice will be playing Joseph the er –

MAURICE. – Joseph. Thank you.

RONALD. Thank you.

They run offstage.

Bethlehem – stable

From the distance we hear:

JOSEPH. Not far now, Josephine. It's just there. That stable under the stars.

Enter RONALD *as the* MIDWIFE. *In midwife hat and cape and riding a bicycle. She glides across the stage. Exits.*

LOUD CRASH.

JOSEPH *bows his head and enters the stable. He looks down at* MARY. MARY *is a pool of light. Tentatively he approaches the pool of light.*

Mary? Look, Mary. I called the midwife.

MIDWIFE *enters. She bows her head and enters the stable. Looks down at* MARY.

MIDWIFE. Hello, Mary. I'm Josephine. Now I'm just going to lie you down.

Mimes lying MARY *down.*

JOSEPH. She's just going to lie you down, Mary.

MIDWIFE. So I can make a quick examination –

JOSEPH. So she can make a quick examination –

MIDWIFE. Would you get some straw, Joseph, to put under Mary's back to make her more comfortable.

JOSEPH. Certainly.

He looks round for straw.

Um –

MIDWIFE. Outside in the straw store.

JOSEPH. In the what?

MIDWIFE. Straw store.

JOSEPH. Straw store?

MIDWIFE. Yes please.

JOSEPH. Just going to the straw store, Mary.

JOSEPH *goes outside.*

SFX: Crickets. Goats. Hens. Night sounds.

He looks for the straw store. Suddenly looks up at the night. Gasps.

Music:

Look! It's a huge star! It has been followin' us and now it has stopped. It's shining down. And all about it, the stars and planets and constellations and all the swirling galaxies and nebulae! They have also halted in their heavenly motions. And – the winds have ceased. And the leaves on the trees. And there is no sound of any water or running rivers heard. And look!

All the clocks have stopped ticking. And the stable lad is fast asleep with his horses and the chambermaid on the bed she was making and the pastry-cook snoring into the cake bowl and the dogs curled up on the stairs and the cats and mice lying side by side.

SFX: Night sounds stop.

MIDWIFE. There is a great silence.

JOSEPH. The hour is come.

They stand in the silence.

MIDWIFE. Hurry with the straw, Joseph!

JOSEPH (*jumps to*). Right! Sorry yes. The straw.

Mimes being given some straw.

Thank you.

Comes back into the stable. Realises. GASPS.

Agh! Midwife?

MIDWIFE. Yes?

JOSEPH. The ox just gave me some straw. In his hoof!

MIDWIFE. Yes very probably. Now put it under Mary's back would you, Joseph?

JOSEPH. Right. Certainly.

Looks down at MARY.

Nice soft straw, Mary.

JOSEPH *gently puts the straw under* MARY's *back. The* MIDWIFE *proceeds with her examination.*

MIDWIFE. Right. So the head is engaged and the waters have broken.

JOSEPH. Really?

MIDWIFE. The waters have broken and – we're into second-stage labour here.

JOSEPH. Is that bad?

MIDWIFE. No. That's very very good. Now then I want you to breathe deeply, Mary. You can help, Joseph. Breathe with her. In through the nose and out through the mouth. Breathe together. Good. Now I'll just make a further examination. The er – cervix is now fully diluted –

JOSEPH. Dilated.

MIDWIFE. Dilated.

JOSEPH. Is it?

MIDWIFE (*demonstrates about a foot*). A good ten centimetres, yes.

JOSEPH. Really!?

MIDWIFE. And the head is ready to crown.

The MIDWIFE *becomes* RONALD.

RONALD. What's that mean then? Ready to crown?

MAURICE. Sorry?

RONALD. Ready to crown?

MAURICE. Ready to crown?

RONALD. Yes.

MAURICE. Erm – well it means – er –

Stands up. Steps over MARY.

Excuse me. It means the baby –

Lies down in a fetal position.

– has now erm left the 'womb' and is proceeding down the 'birth canal'. So now he's er –

Propels himself across the stage.

– pushing, pushing to come out. To come out –

RONALD. – head-first.

MAURICE. Yes. That is if you come out head first. If you're a 'breech' birth of course you come out –

He spins round.

RONALD. Bum-first.

MAURICE. Yes.

RONALD. Cos you were a breech birth, weren't you, Maurice?

MAURICE. I was actually yes as it happens. I've often felt
that's been a major factor in my own life, which has not been
without its stressful moments as you know. In fact –

MIDWIFE. That'll do, Joseph. Would you lower the lights
a little please so that the baby's entry into the world can be
as gentle as possible.

JOSEPH. Certainly. Sorry.

Stage lights fade.

MIDWIFE. Thank you, Joseph.

JOSEPH (*looks up. Gasps*). But – but I'm not – not doing
nothing. The lights is lowering by themselves. And look!

(*Points round the audience.*) Hundreds of birds there look.
All lined up. Watching. Waiting. Robins and blue-tits and
blackbirds and thrushes. And there look! Rabbits and
hedgehogs and foxes and squirrels and badgers and even –
(*At* MRS F*'s feet.*) little hamster there, look.

MIDWIFE. Yes it's like a little menagerie in here. Now then,
Joseph!

JOSEPH. Yes?

MRS F *hums under the ensuing scene.*

Song 6: Holst, 'In the Bleak Midwinter'

MIDWIFE. She's having her main attractions so she's going to
be in a lot of pain. I want you to hold her hand.

JOSEPH. Dunno what to do! Dunno what to do! I feel the
weight of the world upon me! I can't deal with this! It's too
much for me!

MIDWIFE. This is not your moment, Joseph. This is a woman's moment.

JOSEPH. Right. Sorry.

MIDWIFE. Now then – grip Joseph's hand, Mary.

Gives JOSEPH MARY*'s hand.*

JOSEPH. Right.

MIDWIFE. Right now, Joseph, lift Mary up, Joseph. So she can partake more fully in the birth.

JOSEPH. Right right. I'm just lifting you up, Mary.

JOSEPH *mimes lifting* MARY. *He supports her back. The* MIDWIFE *takes* MARY*'s hands. The baby begins to be born.*

MIDWIFE. Now, Mary, can you feel that? Can you feel the head? Look! Here's the head now.

JOSEPH. Oh look! Yes! Look, Mary, it's a little –

MIDWIFE. Quiet, Joseph! Now breathe, Mary! Push. Push. Breathe. Breathe. Breathe with her, Joseph! In – out – in – out!

JOSEPH *breathes loudly with* MARY. *In out – in out – in out – in out – in out.*

Good good! And breathe with him, Mary, breathe! Good. Push! Push! Keep pushing. Push the pain away.

JOSEPH. You need to push, Mary! Push! PUSH!

MARY *gives him an earful.*

Alright!

(*To* MIDWIFE.) She is pushing!

MIDWIFE. Good. Good. Now breathe the pain away. Push the pain away! BREATHE the pain away! Good! Good! And the head has been born!

JOSEPH (*gasps in amazement!*). A little baby head, look!

MIDWIFE. And here come the shoulders!

JOSEPH. Little baby shoulders now look!

MIDWIFE. Good good. Breathe and push, breathe and push!
And here comes the rest of him. Good. Good. Push. Push.
Push. Push. Push. Push and –

She glides the baby out. Raises him high into the air.
MIDWIFE *becomes* RONALD.

JOSEPH *becomes* MAURICE. *They look up at the newborn
baby in amazement.*

RONALD. Oh! It's a little baby. A little boy. Isn't he sweet?
Well done Mary.

MAURICE. Well done, Mary.

RONALD. Would you like to take him now, Maurice?

MAURICE. Oh. I would yes.

MAURICE *takes the baby.*

Well done Mary.

RONALD. Cos we're not going to 'cut the cord', are we,
Maurice?

MAURICE. No, Ronald. In order to retain the –

RONALD. Organic connection with the mother!

MAURICE. Right.

RONALD. You'd better lay him on Mary's tummy then so she
can stroke him.

MAURICE. Right yes. Sorry.

He lays the baby on MARY*'s tummy. He is* JOSEPH *again.*
JOSEPH *gazes at* MARY *and her newborn baby.*

JOSEPH. Like a fish running before the surf, our baby was born
into the world, Mary.

RONALD *puts on his veil. Becomes* MARY *holding the
baby.* MAURICE *becomes* JOSEPH *sitting beside her.*

MRS F *sings*.

Song 7: 'Silent Night'

MRS F *bows to the couple. She exits*.

Music: dramatic.

RONALD *exits. He runs back on, pulling on his* WISE MAN *costume*.

The Road from Bethlehem

RONALD. Quick quick, Balthasar the Wise Man! I can hear them! Listen! Herod's armies are coming! By land, by sea, and by air! We must find the baby and the baby's baby family!

He runs off. Runs back.

He sees MAURICE *has not moved*.

Quick quick, Balthasar the Wise Man! I can hear them! Listen! Herod's armies are –

Still MAURICE *does not move*.

Quick, Balthasar! We must warn 'em before it is too late and save the baby! Quick to our camels and save the baby!

He rushes out. Runs back. MAURICE *still hasn't moved*.

Music cuts.

Maurice? You're meant to be a Wise Man! Balthasar the Wise!

MAURICE. I've rather lost the will to continue, Ronald.

RONALD. Pardon?

MAURICE. I've been thinking about what you and Mrs F was saying about me in the dressing rooms. And I'm sure a lot of it is very true. And I realise here am I trying to write a show about – healing.

RONALD. Ealing?

MAURICE. Healing! And I'm not even healed myself.

RONALD. Um –

MAURICE. I believe there is a spiritual world, Ronald. Inside us. I believe that round every living thing there is a halo of light. We are divine beings, Ronald, and do not know it. That's what it's about, the Birth Scene. The bringing to birth of that divine part of ourselves, that inner divine child, which can heal ourselves, and heal the whole world, Ronald!

RONALD. Well, that's alright then, isn't it?

MAURICE. No!! Cos when I look for my divine part, my inner divine child, what do I see?

RONALD. What do you see, Maurice?

MAURICE. A great black toad, Ronald.

RONALD. A great black toad?

MAURICE. Inside me!

RONALD. It's all them diets you been on, Maurice! You got very strange on the five and nine.

MAURICE. Five and two!

RONALD. That was worse!

MAURICE. Exactly. That's what it feels like to be me, Ronald! Inside me! Picture yourself inside me, Ronald.

RONALD. I don't think I can do that, Maurice.

MAURICE. I know I'm a child of creation. A perfect pristine being within the universe. But I seen my toad, Ronald. I know it's there! Hopping up and down. Always there! Hoppin'! And I hate my toad. I know I should love my toad. Learn to accept my toad. I know I should do that. So I do. I lavish it with love and attention. But it just gets worse. Lolloping about! Causing havoc. Causing untold damage! I'm damaged goods, Ronald! Not surprising she left me.

RONALD. Norman?

MAURICE. Maureen!

RONALD. Mormon?

MAURICE. Maureen!!

RONALD. Maureen!!!

MAURICE (*tearful*). Look at me, Ronnie! I've spent a fortune on self-help! But I'm just a spiritual Hoover demonstrator, hacking about on the fringes of eternal truth. I'm just a very very horrible person, Ronald!

He breaks down sobbing.

RONALD. What's happening, Maurice? Maurice?

MAURICE. What's it look like's happening!? I'm having a breakdown, Ronald!!

(*Sobs.*) I'm completely – confused!!

RONALD. Well, Maurice, you know what they say?

MAURICE. What?

RONALD. Enlightenment is the highest form of confusion.

MAURICE *falls on the stage, sobs even louder.*

MAURICE. I am not worthy of our story here tonight, Ronald!

(*Sobs.*) I've never felt so low.

(*Sobs.*) I wish I'd never been born.

He keels over.

RONALD. Er – ladies and gentlemen, I never seen my friend in a state of such utter devastation.

Heart-rending sobs from MAURICE. RONALD *thinks.*

So – er – you know that bit in *Peter Pan* when Tinker Bell is dying and everyone has to stop her dyin' by clapping to prove they believe in fairies –

MAURICE *keels over onto his back. Lies motionless.*

Well, I think we're going to have to do something similar for
my friend to save him from a dreadful spiritual death. I'd
never normally ask this of an audience during a show – but
could you give him – well – a big round of applause?

Audience applaud or cheer. MAURICE *doesn't move.*

Thank you. Um – the thing is – he likes more. Whistles,
cheers, stamping and bravos. Could you send waves of
loving and caring into Maurice's heart. So – if you would
please for my sake – give him a big one for me.

Applause. Bravos and whistles.

MAURICE *moves. He looks at* RONALD.

It seems to have worked. Thank you very much! Are you
feeling better now, Maurice?

MAURICE. A little bit better, yes Ronald.

RONALD. Would you like to get up off the floor now, Maurice?

MAURICE. Right-oh.

RONALD *gives* MAURICE *his hand. Helps him up.*

Ronnie?

RONALD. Yes?

MAURICE. Would you do something for me, Ronnie?

RONALD. Anything, Maurice. What would you like to do?

MAURICE. The angel scene. Where I play Gabriel.

RONALD. Again?

MAURICE. Yes.

RONALD. Right. I'll get the chair.

Fetches the chair.

So you stand on the chair, Maurice. Stand on this chair.

MAURICE *stands on the chair.* RONALD *puts on his veil.*

RONALD. And I'll be Mary.

MAURICE. Right.

RONALD. So which bit would you like to go from?

MAURICE. The bit when he tells her about the little tiny little baby. The little baby boy.

RONALD. Right. I'll stand here then.

MAURICE. And I'll stand here.

RONALD. Right.

MAURICE. Right.

Becomes GABRIEL, *whooshes his wings.*

Music.

Mary? Mary? Mary?

RONALD. What? What? What?

MAURICE. Blessed are you above all women. And all men.

RONALD. Am I? Why?

MAURICE. Cos you shall conceive a son.

RONALD. Oh good.

MAURICE. And you shall call his name Wonderful, Marvellous, Peace-Maker, Councillor, Magical, Triffic, Brill, Beautiful. And you will love him.

RONALD. Will I?

MAURICE. Yes!!! You will love him! *You will love him!*

RONALD. Yes! Alright! I will! *I will love him!*

MAURICE. Even if he's mean? Even if he deliberately scares his best friend into thinking he's trapped in a horrible tiny little dark room, playing on his innate claustrophobic fears of primal entrapment and makes him run away? Even then?

Music: fades.

RONALD *looks at* MAURICE.

RONALD. Would you like to get off the chair now, Maurice?

Gives him his hand. MAURICE *gets off the chair.*

Have you got a hanky?

MAURICE. It's at the laundry.

RONALD *mops* MAURICE's *brow with the hem of his robe.* MAURICE *blows his nose on it.*

RONALD. Maurice?

MAURICE. Yes?

RONALD. I love you, Maurice. And I won't ever leave you.

MAURICE. Ever?

RONALD. Ever. Come here, Maurice.

MAURICE *steps towards him.* RONALD *hugs him.*

MRS F *enters and sees them hugging.*

MRS F. Oh!

RONALD. Hello, Mrs F. It's Mrs F, Maurice.

MAURICE. Hello, Mrs F.

RONALD. We're goin' on with the show, Mrs F. Aren't we, Maurice?

MAURICE. We're getting on with the show, Mrs F!

MRS F. Good. Come along then.

RONALD. Sorry I shouted at you, Mrs F. And Maurice is sorry too. For what he done. Aren't you, Maurice?

MAURICE. I am yes.

RONALD. Your singin' is like an angel, Mrs F. In fact listnin' to your singin' we thought you was one. Didn't we, Maurice? Maurice?

MAURICE. We could not have done what we done without what you done.

RONALD. Beautifully put, Maurice.

MAURICE. Thank you.

MRS F. Thank you.

MAURICE. Thank *you*.

Music: Pastoral, Beethoven 6th.

RONALD. And now the little holy family have their first little breakfast.

MRS F. I don't think so. Cut to the shepherds!

RONALD. The shepherds?

MAURICE. The shepherds?

MRS F. The shepherds! I've got a train to catch.

(*Sings.*) There were shepherds abiding in the –

Suddenly MAURICE *sees the little town is still revealed.*

MAURICE. Town!

MRS F. Town?!

MAURICE. The town! THE TOWN! Do the handle! Do the handle!

RONALD *rushes upstage looking for the handle.*

RONALD. DO THE HANDLE?! DO THE HANDLE?!

MAURICE. THE HANDLE! THE HANDLE!!!

MRS F (*bursts into song*).
    'HALLELUJAH! HALLELU– '

MAURICE. No No! Not the Handel! The HANDLE!

RONALD. I'M DOING THE HANDLE!

MRS F. *I'M DOING THE HANDEL!*

MAURICE. Do the song, Mrs F! –

MRS F. 'HALLELUJAH! HALLELU– '

MAURICE. NO! The sheep song, Mrs F! Rock and sheep, Ronald!

RONALD *and* MAURICE *exit stage and run back with the cosmic rock, two stuffed sheep and a toy lamb. They drop the rock in place.*

Song 8: Handel, 'There Were Shepherds Abiding in the Field'

MRS F (*sings*).
There were shepherds abiding in the field, keeping watch over their flock by night.

MRS F *finishes song. Bows and exits.*

Bethlehem – Fields

SFX: Sheep sounds.

MAURICE *and* RONALD *are sitting on the rock.* RONALD *is the* YOUNG SHEPHERD. MAURICE *is the* OLDER SHEPHERD.

The YOUNG SHEPHERD *starts playing on a tuneless pipe. The* OLDER SHEPHERD *examines one of the stuffed lambs. The* YOUNG SHEPHERD *plays on and on and on.* OLDER SHEPHERD *can take it no more.*

OLDER SHEPHERD. Excuse me.

YOUNG SHEPHERD. Yes?

OLDER SHEPHERD. Would you mind keeping the noise down a bit.

YOUNG SHEPHERD. Right.

YOUNG SHEPHERD *stops blowing the pipe.* OLDER SHEPHERD *keeps examining lamb.*

I thought I saw an angel today.

OLDER SHEPHERD. Did you?

YOUNG SHEPHERD. In the crevice behind that hill.

OLDER SHEPHERD. Really?

YOUNG SHEPHERD. D'you think I did see an angel?

OLDER SHEPHERD. What did it look like?

YOUNG SHEPHERD. It was sort of light and like a fluttering of cloth against a bush.

OLDER SHEPHERD. Probably a bit of cloth stuck in a bush.

YOUNG SHEPHERD. Probably.

> OLDER SHEPHERD *examines the sheep.* YOUNG SHEPHERD *blows pipe again.*

Sorry! Sorry!

Puts pipe down.

Do you think I'll ever see an angel?

OLDER SHEPHERD. Well, they are very rare now.

YOUNG SHEPHERD. Rarer than they used to be?

OLDER SHEPHERD. Yes.

YOUNG SHEPHERD. Did one ever appear to your father?

OLDER SHEPHERD. No.

YOUNG SHEPHERD. Did one ever appear to your grandfather?

OLDER SHEPHERD. No.

YOUNG SHEPHERD. Did one ever appear to his father?

OLDER SHEPHERD. No.

YOUNG SHEPHERD. Or his father before –

OLDER SHEPHERD. No!

YOUNG SHEPHERD. So we ain't really got a dog's chance then, have we?

OLDER SHEPHERD. We haven't, to be honest.

YOUNG SHEPHERD. Do you think you have to be in a special state of mind to see an angel? I mean do you think I try too hard to see an angel? Should I just stop thinking about it?

OLDER SHEPHERD. I do really, to be honest.

YOUNG SHEPHERD *takes this in.*

Don't mind my sayin' that?

YOUNG SHEPHERD. No no.

Pause.

Have you ever been on holiday?

OLDER SHEPHERD. Um – had a weekend break last year.

YOUNG SHEPHERD. Where was that then?

OLDER SHEPHERD. Dead Sea. Bit quiet.

YOUNG SHEPHERD. See any angels at the sea?

OLDER SHEPHERD. Er no.

YOUNG SHEPHERD. Probably get their wings damp.

OLDER SHEPHERD. Right.

YOUNG SHEPHERD (*points to stuffed sheep*). Wendy's got a bit of a limp on her, hasn't she?

OLDER SHEPHERD. She has yes.

YOUNG SHEPHERD. Is there anything we can do?

OLDER SHEPHERD. Well, I generally rub on the saps and barks of various trees.

YOUNG SHEPHERD. Shall I go and get some saps and barks?

OLDER SHEPHERD. No, I already done it, thanks.

YOUNG SHEPHERD. Right-oh.

OLDER SHEPHERD. D'you want to count the sheep?

YOUNG SHEPHERD. Oh yes please!!!

OLDER SHEPHERD. Okay!

YOUNG SHEPHERD. Okay! Where do I start?

OLDER SHEPHERD. Right. Start by the ridge, go down the river bank, past the bushy topped tree then long the escarpment and round the back.

YOUNG SHEPHERD. Will we have something to eat when I get back?

OLDER SHEPHERD. Couple of falafels?

YOUNG SHEPHERD. *Falafels!!!? My favourite!!! Falafels!!!*

Okay! Off now!!

Leaps up. Turns suddenly.

What if you see an angel?

OLDER SHEPHERD. I won't see an angel.

YOUNG SHEPHERD. But you'll tell me if you do?

OLDER SHEPHERD. I will yes.

YOUNG SHEPHERD. Promise?

OLDER SHEPHERD. Promise!

YOUNG SHEPHERD. Okay!

OLDER SHEPHERD. Okay!

The YOUNG SHEPHERD *exits. We hear him counting into the distance.*

YOUNG SHEPHERD. Number one. Number two. Number three. Number four…

The OLDER SHEPHERD *sighs with relief. The counting fades away.*

An ANGEL *appears behind the first shepherd. It is* RONALD *wearing wings.*

ANGEL. Shepherd? I'm an angel!!!

OLDER SHEPHERD. Keep counting the sheep!

The ANGEL *leaps on to the rock.*

ANGEL. Shepherd! I am an angel!!!

OLDER SHEPHERD *turns and gasps. He shields his eyes from the celestial light.*

OLDER SHEPHERD. Of the Lord?

ANGEL. Of the Lord.
Fear Not!
I have only joy to give you.
There is a child born.
And I'll tell you the sign.
How you will know him.
You will find a baby.
In a manger in a cave
Full of light.
And there will be a load of animals and birds and Wise Men in there giving gifts and making speeches. But you push your way to the front and if you've got a baby lamb spare, that'd go down nicely.

The ANGEL *flaps his wings and whooshes off. The* OLDER SHEPHERD *remains transfixed.*

From the distance we hear the YOUNG SHEPHERD *returning.*

YOUNG SHEPHERD. Number seventy-five... number-seventy six...

YOUNG SHEPHERD *enters. He counts the last three sheep.*

Seventy-seven, seventy-eight, seventy-nine, number eighty. Eighty.

He sits down happily.

Hungry now! Falafels! Lovely!

OLDER SHEPHERD *looks at him.*

What? What!?

OLDER SHEPHERD. I don't know how to tell you this.

YOUNG SHEPHERD. What?

OLDER SHEPHERD. I just seen an angel.

The YOUNG SHEPHERD *takes this in.*

YOUNG SHEPHERD. Oh No!!!!!!! And I missed it!!!!!!

OLDER SHEPHERD. I would have asked him to hang on but – glory shone all about.

YOUNG SHEPHERD. This is a very great disappointment to me.

OLDER SHEPHERD. There was light and singing and the whole sky was humming with the sound of wings. There was great swirling lights and colours bursting up into the sky. It was like – fireworks night! Or the Olympics! I never seen nothin like it!

YOUNG SHEPHERD. What did he say?

OLDER SHEPHERD. Sorry?

YOUNG SHEPHERD. Did he say anything about – me at all?

OLDER SHEPHERD. Who?

YOUNG SHEPHERD. The angel?

OLDER SHEPHERD. Oh – well – no – he didn't mention you specifically by name no.

YOUNG SHEPHERD. Right.

OLDER SHEPHERD. He said – hang on! I remember now! Yes! He says we got to go to –

(*Remembering.*) – Bethlehem!

YOUNG SHEPHERD. Bethlehem?

Music.

OLDER SHEPHERD. To find a baby!

YOUNG SHEPHERD. A baby? What kind of baby?

OLDER SHEPHERD. I dunno. A baby! A baby who will – who will – yes that's it! Heal the whole world!

YOUNG SHEPHERD. Heal the whole world!!!?

OLDER SHEPHERD. A Messiah!!!

YOUNG SHEPHERD. So – is that like an angel then, a Messiah?

OLDER SHEPHERD. No. It's in a – a completely different league really. It's like – comparing the sound of the first bumble-bee – (*Thinks.*) to a full summer's day.

YOUNG SHEPHERD. So better than an angel then?

OLDER SHEPHERD. Yeah!!!!

YOUNG SHEPHERD. Well we'd better go there then! To Bethlehem!

OLDER SHEPHERD. Hang on!

YOUNG SHEPHERD. What?

OLDER SHEPHERD. We need a baby lamb! That's what he said!

YOUNG SHEPHERD (*panicking*). Baby lamb!!?? Baby lamb!!?? Where we going to get a baby lamb from!!??

OLDER SHEPHERD. We're shepherds!

YOUNG SHEPHERD. Oh yes. Sorry.

OLDER SHEPHERD. Look!

Chooses person from audience.

Here's a baby lamb.

YOUNG SHEPHERD. Yes. So there is. Hello, baby lamb. What's your name? Sorry? Are you coming to Bethlehem? Really? Oh good! Come on then! Come on!

They all run round the stage.

Music: Builds.

OLDER SHEPHERD (*to lamb*). Bet you didn't expect this when you bought a ticket. Wait wait!!!

They skid to a stop.

YOUNG SHEPHERD. What what!!??

OLDER SHEPHERD (*points to the star*). Look! Look! Up there! Up there!

YOUNG SHEPHERD (*looks up*). Oh yes!

(*To lamb*.) Look look, baby lamb! Can you see that? Mind your eyes!

They all look up at the star that glows bright. They all shield their eyes.

OLDER SHEPHERD. Star of wonder! Star of light!

YOUNG SHEPHERD. Why, it must be Christmas night!

OLDER SHEPHERD. No not Christmas night, whate'er you say. It can only be –

BOTH. Christmas Day!!!!!

Song 9: Handel, Chorus – 'Hallelujah!'

MRS F *is revealed. Transformed into an angel, clothed in white with golden wings. She joins in with the chorus.*

Snow falls on the stage.

Snow falls on the audience.

The End.